COLORADO
MOUNTAIN CLUB
PACK GUIDE

THE BEST HIKES ON THE
Continental Divide Trail:
COLORADO

D0992853

**CONTINENTAL DIVIDE TRAIL COALITION,
WITH LIZ THOMAS**

The Colorado Mountain Club Press
Golden, Colorado

The Best Hikes on the Continental Divide Trail: Colorado
© 2016 by Continental Divide Trail Coalition

PUBLISHED BY

The Colorado Mountain Club Press
710 Tenth Street, Suite 200, Golden, Colorado 80401
303-996-2743   e-mail: cmcpress@cmc.org

Founded in 1912, The Colorado Mountain Club is the largest outdoor recreation, education, and conservation organization in the Rocky Mountains. Look for our books at your local bookstore or outdoor retailer or online at www.cmc.org/store.

Liz Thomas and Karl Luce: authors
Teresa Martinez and Josh Shusko: contributors
Jerry Brown: surveyor and cartographer
Kerry Shakarjian, Caitlin Reusch, and Guthrie Alexander: maps
John Gascoyne: series editor
Eduard B. Avis: copy editor
Erika K. Arroyo: design, composition, and production
Sarah Gorecki: publisher

CONTACTING THE PUBLISHER
We would appreciate it if readers would alert us to any errors or outdated information by contacting us at the address above.

DISTRIBUTED TO THE BOOK TRADE BY
The Mountaineers Books, 1001 SW Klickitat Way, Suite 201, Seattle, WA 98134, 800-553-4453, www.mountaineersbooks.org

Topographic maps were created using CalTopo software (caltopo.com).

COVER PHOTO: Deb "Walking Carrot" Hunsicker on the Continental Divide Trail west of Berthoud Pass. Photo by Phil "Nowhere Man" Hough

We gratefully acknowledge the financial support of the people of Colorado through the Scientific and Cultural Facilities District of greater Denver for our publishing activities.

WARNING: Although there has been an effort to make the trail descriptions in this book as accurate as possible, some discrepancies may exist between the text and the trails in the field. Hiking in mountainous areas—and canyons and deserts as well—is a high-risk activity. This guidebook is not a substitute for your experience and common sense. The users of this guidebook assume full responsibility for their own safety. Weather, terrain conditions, and individual abilities must be considered before undertaking any of the hikes in this guide.

First Edition

ISBN 978-1-937052-29-4
Ebook 978-1-937052-30-0

Printed in Korea

A hearty thanks to all my hiking partners, especially Felicia "Princess of Darkness" Hermosillo, Samantha "Aroo" Mills, and CDTC Trail Operations Manager Val Sokolowski, who helped me ground truth the hikes in this book. Val also worked with volunteers and trail builders and adopters to make sure that this book incorporated the perspectives not only of hikers, but also of those who work to ensure this trail exists for future generations. I am grateful for all those who have worked to build, maintain, and protect this trail over the years.

Many thanks to all the photographers. Your eagerness to share the beauty of the CDT with others is what keeps this trail alive: Johnny "Bigfoot" Carr, Lawton "Disco" Grinter, Phil "Nowhere Man" Hough, Nancy "Why Not?!" Huber, Annie MacWilliams, Steven "Twinkle" Shattuck, Lance Stack, and Peter "Czech" Sustr.

May a cooler of cold sodas find their way to the CDT Class of 2015 and all the other hikers I consulted with. I want to especially call out Steven "Twinkle" Shattuck and Johnny "Bigfoot" Carr, whose photos in this book and on our many hikes continue to rock my socks off.

May many Diet Cokes find their way to "Buck 30," who ground truthed hikes for me, particularly the Parkview Mountain hike. If you get lost there, send all complaints to him.

Thank you to Phil "Nowhere Man" Hough and Deb "Walking Carrot" Hunsicker for the cover photo and numerous other photos, and for cheering me up in the Great Basin in Wyoming when I first met you on the CDT in 2010.

Deepest thanks from every hiker and me to Jerry Brown, whose constantly updated maps and data points provided the basis for the trail information. Your hard work is appreciated and I'll never forget our first meeting in Helena National Forest.

Lastly, I dedicate this pack guide to Brian "Mr. Gorbachev" Davidson and our animal and plant creatures. Thank you for the freedom to go hiking for months at a time, summer after summer. Your kindness, patience, generosity, and enthusiasm have made this book possible.

—*Liz Thomas*

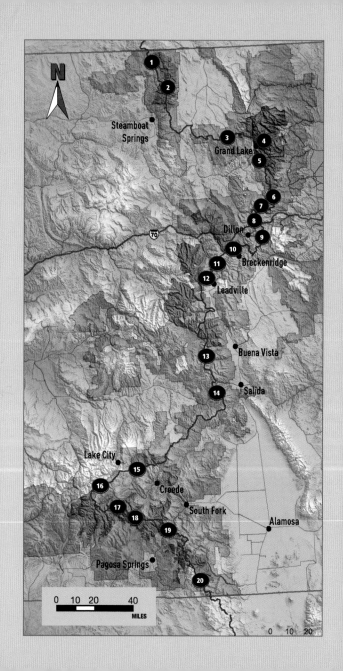

CONTENTS

A sign marks where the trail to Herman Lake breaks off from the CDT.

ACKNOWLEDGMENTS

For the past year, the CMC pack guide team has been a constant presence in my life, email inbox, and CDTC cubicle. I have had a great team who has nurtured me, mentored me, and kept me in line and I greatly appreciate the guidance I received.

I am enormously grateful to John Gascoyne, my field editor, whose rich knowledge of the Colorado mountains (not to mention English grammar) made my writing stronger and easier for readers to digest. You may not have always had faith in my ability to finish this book, but you diligently edited whatever I gave you with good humor. Your thoughtful comments were appreciated. Thank you, John.

I would also like to thank CMC Press; my publisher Sarah Gorecki; our map wizards Kerry Shakarjian, Caitlin Reusch, and Guthrie Alexander; CDTC volunteer Karl Luce; and CDTC Executive Director Teresa Martinez. Sarah's ability to keep me on deadline and think of the book as a whole was very helpful. The maps brought my words to life and helped me catch my errors along the way. Karl created a foundation for this book and contributed to the Monarch Pass hike. Most important, this book would not have been possible without Teresa's vision for the trail and her encyclopedic knowledge of every pass and trail crossing. Her faith in the value of this book has made this a reality.

Lastly, I would like to thank my colleagues at the CDTC, including Val Sokolowski and Peter Sustr, and to the many volunteers, trail builders, and maintainers who have worked to complete the CDT. Without your hard work, I would have had no trail to write about.

—Liz Thomas

Surreal beauty of early season bloom in the forest along the CDT.　PHOTO BY JOHNNY "BIGFOOT" CARR

Introduction

Considered one of the greatest long-distance trails in the world, the Continental Divide Trail (CDT) extends 3,100 miles from Mexico to Canada. It is the highest, most challenging, and most remote of our thirteen National Scenic Trails. Ranging from 4,200 to 14,270 feet in elevation, the CDT provides a variety of recreational activities to many hundreds of thousands of people each year, including hiking, horseback riding, cross-country skiing, snowshoeing, wildlife viewing, fishing, hunting, and sightseeing.

In Colorado, the CDT stretches about 800 miles—from the Rio Grande National Forest near New Mexico to the Routt National Forest near Wyoming. It passes through Rocky Mountain National Park, seven national forests, and eleven federally designated wilderness areas. The CDT in Colorado is at or above 11,000 feet for 70 miles and is home to Grays Peak—at 14,270 feet the highest point on any National Scenic Trail in the nation.

The Continental Divide Trail Coalition

The Continental Divide Trail Coalition (CDTC) is the 501(c)(3) national nonprofit working to create a community committed to constructing, promoting, and protecting in perpetuity the CDT, which stretches from Canada to Mexico, through Montana, Idaho, Wyoming, Colorado, and New Mexico. Trail enthusiasts passionate about the Continental Divide National Scenic Trail (CDT) formed the CDTC in June of 2012. They recognized there was a need for a national advocacy group to continue the legacy of stewardship, and they were determined to ensure the CDT not languish because of limited funding and public engagement. The CDTC is made up of volunteers, recreationists, trail supporters, and natural resource professionals who have the desire to build upon the strengths and successes of the past and pick up where others left off. They seek to build strong alliances with the many other local regional groups that care about the CDT and to build a strong national and international community with the sole mission of preserving the CDT.

CDTC is recognized by the US Forest Service, Bureau of Land Management, and the National Park Service as the lead national partner in the stewardship of the CDT and is involved in trail planning, scouting and construction, fundraising, advocacy, volunteer recruitment and coordination, distribution of public information, education, and conservation of the trail and its corridor. Most important, CDTC is creating a long-term trail culture that will love, support, and protect the trail not only today but for future generations.

Protecting the CDT is considered one of the largest continuing conservation efforts in the history of the United States. The trail is much more than just a line on a map—it is a living museum of the American West, a place to reconnect with nature, and a unifying force bringing together multitudes of different people. As of 2015, 90 percent of the CDT is on dedicated hiking trails. But this means 10 percent of the CDT is co-aligned with roads—places shared with motor vehicles, which can be dangerous for nonmotorized users. Of the 800 miles of the CDT in Colorado, 120 have yet to be moved away from roads. Colorado is home to one of the priority "gap areas"—areas of incomplete trail—on the CDT: Muddy Pass, which uses 16 miles of highway to connect two sections of trail. With few exceptions, the hikes in this book are in areas closed to motorized vehicles and are models of the ideal—what the trail could look like when it is completed.

Since the CDT was designated a National Scenic Trail by Congress in 1978, volunteers, staff, land managers, and locals have united to plan, route, build, and maintain the CDT. In 2012, the Continental Divide Trail Coalition (CDTC) was formed as a 501(c)(3) national nonprofit working in partnership with the US Forest Service, the National Park Service, and the Bureau of Land Management to protect, promote, and preserve the CDT. One of the major goals of the Coalition is to get the CDT off roads and into safer and more scenic areas.

Whether you want to hike one mile or do the entire 3,100 miles, we urge you to enjoy this wonderful, world-class resource and to share it with others. When you finish your hike, send us some photos and tell us about your experience. We'll share much of this information to inspire others to get connected to the CDT. If you enjoy your time on the CDT as much as we have, consider becoming a CDTC member, volunteering to build or maintain the trail, or attending one of the CDTC's special events, which are held throughout the year.

Have a great time out there and be safe. Read the hiking tips in this pack guide and know that you are walking a cherished international resource, one that will last for generations to come.

HOW CDTC CHOSE THE HIKES FOR THIS BOOK

In the process of creating this guide, CDTC surveyed dozens of long-distance CDT hikers, asking, "If you could go back and do a dayhike anywhere on the CDT in Colorado, where would you go?" What's amazing is that these hikers kept mentioning the same places over and over again. The hikes in this book are, thus, highlights of the CDT. These are the places that long-distance hikers —people who might be jaded to natural beauty after walking 3,100 miles from Mexico to Canada—say they would gladly revisit.

The hikes in this book are geographically distributed throughout the state and come in a variety of distances, elevation gain, and levels of accessibility. Although there are certainly hikes in this book that are harder than others, CDTC encourages you to consider all of them, regardless of their difficulty level. The first few miles of some of the longest hikes in this book are entirely suitable for families, those just getting into hiking, and visitors short on time. For most of the hikes, CDTC includes options for those looking for shorter and longer hikes.

> **CDT and volunteers**
>
> Volunteers have been the lifeblood of the CDT and the CDTC from the beginning. They donate their time to be a vital part of this historic undertaking and devote themselves to the hard physical labor necessary to build a trail mile by mile, often trekking miles into the backcountry to arrive at a project site. They build new tread, construct bridges and trailheads, repair eroded and damaged stretches of trail, and scout potential CDT locations. Volunteers are also engaged in community development and education programs that celebrate the trail and all it offers to communities along and around its corridor. If you are interested in learning more about our volunteer programs, please contact us at volunteer@ continentaldividetrail.org.

HOW TO USE THIS GUIDEBOOK

Rather than arranging the hikes alphabetically or by difficulty, hikes are organized geographically, starting with a hike near Steamboat Springs in the north and ending with a hike near Chama, New Mexico, in the south. This was done so that you, the reader, would seriously consider walking every hike in the book, not just those at your current hiking level. No matter how strong a hiker you are, know that any hike in this book can be made as long or as short as you like—just decide for yourself and your party when and where you would like to turn around. Just because a hike is listed as an "overnighter" does not mean that you cannot simply do a one-hour out-and-back hike from the trailhead. These hikes were chosen because they truly are wonderful examples of the beauty, majesty, and diversity of the CDT.

MAPS AND NAVIGATION

The CDT is one trail where you really want to have a good map. Unlike some other long-distance trails, the CDT route and the side trails mentioned in this book are not always marked with signs—especially signs that specifically say "CDT." In addition to a good map, you'll also want to have a decent compass to orient yourself to both the map and the trail descriptions in this guide.

Trails Illustrated Maps, created by National Geographic, are pocket-sized, easy to read, and sold at almost every outdoor store. These provide a great overview map that can help you get to the trailhead and find bailout options when the weather turns bad or an emergency happens. Printed on waterproof paper, these maps are created for the hiker and include useful landmarks such as trailheads, campgrounds, water sources, and established campsites. If you live outside of Colorado and want to plan your hike before leaving home, search for stores close to where you'll be hiking or order your maps online. For more info visit www.natgeomaps.com/trail-maps/trails-illustrated-maps. You may also wish to contact CDTC at either info@continentaldividetrail.org or by calling our office at (303) 996-2759.

Wildflowers dot the trail during the summer.

Bear Creek Survey maps are highly accurate (to the level of every turn and switchback), frequently updated, and reasonably priced. Data for these books was originally collected in partnership and under the supervision of the US Forest Service. You can purchase maps for the entire state in several formats: traditional bound book; unbound, pre-printed maps; or PDFs (print your own maps or upload them to your smartphone or tablet). Bear Creek Survey also sells custom-built SD cards for your GPS, tablet, or phone that are fully loaded with tracks, maps, and waypoints. With enough advance notice, Bear Creek will configure your GPS unit with the data you need. Bear Creek Survey maps can be purchased at www.bearcreeksurvey.com, where you can also download free GPS waypoints. Please note that these maps only show the CDT and the immediate surrounding area. It is suggested you also carry an overview map so that you can have a better knowledge of bailout options.

Guthook's Trail Guide Apps (available for both iPhone and Android) are easy-to-use phone apps that don't require a cell signal but can show where you are on the trail relative to the map. They are based on the Bear Creek Survey data, and include thousands of points of interest along the trail, including water sources, campsites, and views. They also include photos of points of interest and interactive elevation profiles that show how steep or long climbs will be. The apps automatically update when the coders get news of trail re-routes. These can be downloaded from www.guthookhikes.com or the iTunes or Google Play stores. These apps can supplement your knowledge of an area, but PLEASE also carry paper maps. Batteries can die and phones can get lost or wet, and the CDT is not always an easy trail to navigate. Please note that, as with the Bear Creek Survey maps, if you use the Guthook apps you should also carry an overview map.

WHAT DO THE RATINGS MEAN?

CDTC encourages you to try every hike—even if just for a short distance. Although this book lists only 20 hikes, for each hike options are provided for a wide range of hiking levels:

- Family Friendly: Less than 3 miles, with less than 1,000 feet of elevation gain
- Easy: 7–10 miles, with less than 2,000 feet of elevation gain
- Moderate: 7.5–11 miles, with less than 2,000 feet of elevation gain
- Difficult: 10–13 miles, with near to or more than 3,000 feet of elevation gain
- Extreme: 15+ miles with more than 3,000 feet of elevation gain

- Overnighter: 20+ miles, with more than 5,000 feet of elevation gain, best done as an overnight or multi-day trip

For each overnight hike, there is a suggested rating. For example, a rating of "Moderate Overnighter" means that if the hike is done as a two-day trip, each day would be between 7.5 and 11 miles, with less than 2,000 feet elevation gain per day. That same trip, if divided over three days, would become an "Easy Overnighter" trip.

ACCESS

We're not kidding when we say "this trip requires a four-wheel-drive high clearance vehicle." CDTC volunteers recently went out to one of the trailheads listed in this book that is designated "four-wheel-drive access only" and came back with horror stories calling it "the worst road I've ever driven on." That is one of the reasons we chose a good balance of two-wheel-drive and four-wheel-drive accessible trailheads. We too have been stuck on a dirt road and know how frustrating it can be, especially if you would rather be hiking.

It is *highly* advised to call the local Forest Service ranger district before attempting any of the dirt road drives in this book. Many of the roads close during the winter and will not be accessible until the snow melts. Local rangers are quite knowledgeable about what cars have been towed off these roads, and should be able to tell you whether your vehicle can make it through. Most important, rangers can tell you if the roads are muddy. If you are renting a four-wheel-drive vehicle to do one of these hikes, make sure you know how to use it, especially if roads are muddy.

DISTANCE AND ELEVATION GAIN

Distance and elevation gain are always measured in terms of how many miles you will hike and feet you will climb between when you leave your car and when you return.

Liz Thomas looking down towards the trail to Herman Lake.

PHOTO BY LIZ THOMAS

Please note that distances are approximations based on maps and GPS data.

There are three kinds of hikes in this book:

- *Out and Back:* Start at your car, walk to a point, and retrace your steps to return the same way.
- *Loop:* From the trailhead, walk either clockwise or counterclockwise and stay on trail until you are back.
- *Lollipop Loop:* A loop hike with a small out and back component.

For the longer hikes in the book, we provide several options in the Distance section for those who are interested in doing part—but not all—of a hike.

Time to complete was calculated on the assumption that the average hiker will walk 2 miles per hour, plus will need an extra hour for each 1,000 feet of gain.

CAMPING AND BACKPACKING

Although there are several overnight trips listed in the book, almost every hike in this pack guide can be turned into an overnight trip if desired. In many cases, available campsites are suggested. The longer trips can easily be turned into 3–5 day backpacking trips suited to families. Please note that for most of these hikes—especially those in wilderness areas—there are no designated campsites. This means you will have to find your own campsite by picking a flat spot following Leave No Trace principles (see page 23) and staying at least 200 feet away from water sources, trails, and other destination points.

A few hikes in this book (Arapahoe Bay to Knight Ridge and Rocky Mountain National Park Loop) require you to camp at established campsites. You will need to get a permit and make reservations with a ranger. The comments section of these hikes will advise you in this regard.

PERMITS AND FEES

Some hikes in the book require permits for overnight camping. Instructions for getting those permits are included in the Comment section of the hike.

For many of the hikes that go through wilderness areas, you are simply asked to sign in and get a walk-up permit from an unmanned kiosk (this involves filling out a form and attaching it to your pack; this can be done any time of the day). Signing in provides both safety measures for you and critical information for CDT trail managers.

Any overnight camping in Rocky Mountain National Park requires permits and campsite reservations. The instructions for doing this are in the Comment section of each hike. At the time of printing, the fee to enter RMNP was $20 per car for one week.

None of the hikes in this book require any advance permits for dayhiking. A few of the hikes may require you to pay a day use parking fee.

RULES AND REGULATIONS

The CDT goes through some wild places, often in areas at high altitude where plants have a short growing season. Even slight disturbances to plants in the alpine tundra can cause damage that can take hundreds of years to heal.

These guidelines are sometimes the rules in wilderness areas, and they are good camping and hiking practices regardless of where you are in the backcountry:

- Camp at least 200 feet from lakes or streams.
- When camping in alpine basins, use existing campsites.
- Use a stove rather than building a campfire. In wilderness zones, fires must be kept at least 200 feet from water or the trail; in other areas a 100-foot distance is recommended.
- Bury human waste 6 inches deep and 200 feet from water sources.
- Keep your group size below 15 humans or 25 "heartbeats" (including stock animals and dogs). In wilderness areas, there is a maximum of 12 heartbeats.
- Keep dogs leashed or under voice control. Hand-held leashes are required in wilderness areas.
- When hiking on trail, stay on existing routes and never cut switchbacks.
- Walk through mud, snow, or water, not around it. Walking around mud can lead to trail widening.
- Respect posted regulations. Most of the trailheads in this book have information kiosks that list warnings, closures, and rules. Also check with the local Forest Service ranger districts for general information.

FISHING INFORMATION

A few of the hike descriptions mention great fishing spots. A valid Colorado fishing license is required. Single-day licenses can be purchased at many local outfitters.

OTHER USES ON THE TRAIL

Almost all the hikes in this book are on trails open only to nonmotorized users. The Comment section always lets you know what other users you may encounter other than hikers or equestrians. Please yield to other users when necessary and be aware of your surroundings while hiking in areas with mixed use. Bikes should yield to hikers. Hikers should yield to horses. Motorized users should yield to all nonmotorized traffic.

WEATHER ON THE CDT (READ THIS ESPECIALLY IF YOU ARE NEW TO COLORADO)

Thunderstorms are a very real possibility on the Divide and nowhere is that more true than in Colorado. For hikers, this means the possibility of significant exposure to rain, snow, sleet, hail, and lightning. The CDT is often the highest point anywhere around, so lightning is a very real threat for CDT hikers.

Before you go:

Check the weather. If it looks bad, take comfort in knowing that the CDT will always be there. Choose another place to hike, or choose to stick to a lower part of the route that does not go above treeline.

Understand your route. Read your hike description and look at your maps to find out where the exposed areas, ridges, and peaks on your hike are. Use your map to discover where your bailout points may be—side trails that can help get you off a ridge if the weather turns. Then, plan your trip around NOT being in exposed areas during the peak time of day for lightning storms.

The day of your adventure:

Pack for weather and be prepared to turn around. In the Colorado high country, rain, snow, sleet, or hail can happen any day of the year. Bring some extra layers and pack for the right attitude—summiting is optional; coming back alive is not.

Start early. Peak baggers have a rule of thumb to be off summits or exposed areas by noon. The CDT has some long exposed ridge walks, so the earlier you can start, the better you can plan your day according to the weather.

Use your eyes, ears, and hair. Don't rely just on the morning's weather report. If the skies look dark, you are hearing thunder, and the hair on your arms is sticking up, strongly consider a strategic retreat. The trail will be there and waiting for you on a more congenial day.

Do the counting test. Count the seconds (one-Mississippi, two-Mississippi) between when you first see a flash of lightning and when you hear the thunder. If it is less than 30 seconds, take this as a sign to get off the ridge immediately. Keep at least 30 feet between hikers as you retreat. After the storm has passed, wait 30 minutes to return to exposed areas.

During the storm:

Find a safe spot. Lightning generally strikes the highest available point. That is why being on a summit or exposed ridge is a bad idea because YOU become the highest point. Seek lower ground, preferably below treeline in clumps of trees or shrubs of uniform height. Avoid solitary trees, though. Lakes, ponds, and other wet areas can conduct lightning, so it is best to avoid them as well. Although caves or rocky areas may be sheltered from rain, they both can also be dangerous. Crouch low with your feet together and keep a distance of 30 feet from others in your party.

HIKING AT ALTITUDE (READ THIS ESPECIALLY IF YOU ARE NEW TO COLORADO)

Whether you are coming from the mountains, the Front Range, or sea level, for most people it can be a little difficult to breathe on CDT hikes in Colorado. As you go up in altitude, atmospheric pressure drops, meaning there is less oxygen in the air. Hikers have to breathe hard and pump extra blood to compensate.

Acute mountain sickness (also known as altitude sickness) can happen when a hiker climbs to an altitude at a faster rate than his or her body can adjust to changes in atmospheric pressure. Everyone acclimates at different rates.

Symptoms of altitude sickness include headache, dizziness, nausea, shortness of breath, lethargy, and trouble sleeping. Symptoms of advanced altitude sickness include irrational behavior, loss of balance and coordination, vomiting, persistent coughing, and rapid pulse.

To reduce symptoms of altitude sickness:

- If you fly into Denver from a lower elevation, spend a few days doing minimal exercise; e.g., enjoy a sightseeing day and ramp up from there.
- Stay hydrated before you fly, while you are acclimating in town, and especially on the trail. Just because temperatures are cooler at altitude doesn't mean you should drink less. Dehydration and altitude sickness have similar symptoms. Using flavored drink mixes can make drinking enough easier.
- If you are showing symptoms of altitude sickness, immediately descend, hydrate, eat, and rest. If you are showing signs of severe altitude sickness, seek medical attention immediately.

WATER ON THE DIVIDE

According to the U.S. Geological Survey, "A spring is a water resource formed when the side of a hill, a valley bottom or other excavation intersects a flowing body of groundwater at or below the local water table, below which the subsurface material is saturated with water." What this means for the hiker is that there are rarely springs on the Divide, so you will want to carry sufficient amounts with you when you have long ridge walks in alpine areas. Sometimes there are ponds or creeks to be found at low points. You should use your maps to find where there is water along the route and plan your hike, camps, and water carries around water availability.

What to Carry: The Ten Essentials

The Ten Essentials is a list of gear you should carry—regardless of the length of your trip—to help you be fully prepared for every trip and be able to survive the unexpected emergency.

1. **Hydration.** Carry at least two liters or quarts of water on any hike. For arid country or desert hiking, carry more. Keep extra water bottles in your car and drink before and after your hike. Thirst is a sign you are already dehydrated, so drink frequently throughout the day.

2. **Nutrition.** Eat a good breakfast before your hike. Carry snacks and never skip lunch or dinner. Hiking burns a lot of calories. Good decisions are made on full stomachs.

3. **Sun protection.** Sun at high elevation can be intense and a bad sunburn can be uncomfortable and dangerous. Clothes are your first layer of protection. Wear long sleeve shirts, a brimmed hat, and sunglasses. Use sunscreen and lip balm and reapply several times a day.

4. **Insulation.** Weather can change quickly in the high country. Carry a warm hat, gloves, extra socks, and rain/wind jacket on you or in your pack. Cotton retains moisture and does not insulate well; it should not be part of your hiking gear.

5. **Navigation.** Learn to use a map and compass. Your GPS unit or phone app can add to your ability, but is not a substitute. Before a hike, study your route, and the surrounding country, on a good map of the area (our suggested maps are listed for each hike). Refer to the map as needed on the trail.

6. **Illumination.** Include a headlamp or flashlight. Hiking in the dark can be dangerous, but a light can make it somewhat better.

A CDT signpost near Argentine Pass.   PHOTO BY TERESA MARTINEZ

7. **First Aid.** Buy or assemble an adequate first aid kit. I always include blister care, duct tape, and some medications. Tailor your kit to your perceived needs and intended activities.

8. **Fire.** Unless you are carrying a stove for an overnighter, you should only need a fire starter for an intense emergency—but when you need it, you will be very happy you have it. Keep these items dry and ensure that all of them will work in cold or wet weather. If needed, tree sap or dry pine needles can help start a fire.

9. **Repair kit and emergency tools.** A pocket knife or multitool and duct tape are good for various repairs. For emergencies, carry a whistle and signal mirror.

10. **Emergency shelter.** Carry a space blanket and nylon cord or a bivouac sack. Large plastic leaf bags are handy for temporary rain gear, pack covers, or survival shelters.

Keep your distance from the mountain goats on Argentine Pass.

PHOTO BY PHIL "NOWHERE MAN" HOUGH

LEAVE NO TRACE

The Leave No Trace backcountry ethics program was created to encourage sustainable and responsible outdoor use. Follow these guidelines to hike and camp with care for the natural environment you are visiting and help preserve it for future generations. For more information, visit www.lnt.org.

Best practices for Leave No Trace:

- Plan ahead and prepare
- Travel and camp on durable surfaces
- Dispose of waste properly
- Leave what you find—take only photos
- Minimize campfire impacts
- Respect wildlife—view them from a distance
- Be considerate of other visitors

1. Mount Zirkel Wilderness

MAPS	Trails Illustrated, Hahns Peak/ Steamboat Lake, Number 116; Continental Divide Scenic Trail Map Book: Colorado, Bear Creek Survey, Map 86, Segment 43; Guthook App Mile 1519.2 to 1521.4
ELEVATION GAIN	1,250 feet
RATING	Easy
ROUND-TRIP DISTANCE	9.6 miles, with a camping option on the Hare Trail and numerous options on the CDT
ROUND-TRIP TIME	6 hours
NEAREST LANDMARK	Hare Trailhead

COMMENT: If you're looking for a shadier, lower-elevation hike along the CDT, northern Colorado is one of the few places right on the spine of the Continental Divide that is still forested. This hike takes you through fields of wildflowers, open meadows, and conifer forests while offering views of the Mount Zirkel Wilderness. The climb on this hike is gradual and once you reach the Divide, this section is one of the flattest in Colorado.

The Mount Zirkel Wilderness along the Sierra Madre Ridge is usually accessible only by at least a day's walk or by using a four-wheel-drive vehicle. This hike, however, can be started from a two-wheel-drive–accessible trailhead. After parking your car at the trailhead, take the multi-use Hare Trail to quickly and easily gain access. Although many CDT thru-hikers find the Zirkels to be a roller coaster, using the Hare Trail to access the CDT eliminates much of the elevation gain and mileage required to reach the Continental Divide.

The route described here is an out-and-back hike, but it can easily be completed as an overnighter. There are dispersed

The Divide in this section is relatively flat and has many dry camp spots.
PHOTO BY LIZ THOMAS

campsites at the trailhead. There is also a great camping area in a broad meadow about 2.0 miles from the trailhead. Once you reach the CDT, there are numerous dry camps available. However, there is no water on the Divide, so you will want to carry sufficient amounts with you. As the hike goes above treeline at times, check the weather before you go and, should the weather turn, move to lower elevations.

Because the Hare Trail and CDT are open to many uses, keep your eyes peeled for other users. Bikes should yield to hikers. Hikers should yield to horses. Motorized users should yield to all nonmotorized traffic. With this particular hike, though, if you start before 10 a.m., even on weekends, you are unlikely to run into other users.

GETTING THERE: The Hare Trailhead (Trail No. 1199) can be accessed by good dirt roads in a two-wheel-drive vehicle. As the trailhead is relatively high, the road is open only during the summer. The drive to the trailhead is scenic, especially in the fall. Check road conditions before starting.

Felicia "POD" Hermosillo looks at the view from the Divide, which is flat in this section.

PHOTO BY LIZ THOMAS

From the town of Clark, take Colorado Highway 129 for 13.0 miles. Pass Steamboat Lake State Park and continue north. Turn right on the well-marked, wide, and well-graded gravel Forest Service Road 550 and enter Routt National Forest. Take Forest Service Road 550 northeast for 3.7 miles. Follow signs to Forest Service Road 500 and turn right on the wide, well-graded Forest Service Road 500 and follow it northeast for 2.5 miles. Turn right at the sign for Forest Service Road 520, which also should mention the Hare Trailhead. Stay on this well-graded, narrower dirt road for 2.3 miles. Ignore a road on your left and stay on Forest Service Road 520 until the end of the road 0.5 mile later. There are no pit toilets at the Hare Trailhead, but you will pass many trailheads with toilet facilities once you enter Routt National Forest.

THE ROUTE: Take the broad, multi-use Hare Trail (Trail No. 1199) south on generally flat trail for 0.2 mile until it turns east, gradually ascending a hill as you follow a creek below you. The Forest Service has cleared trees in this area, so you will be traveling through meadows of wildflowers. After about 1.5 miles, a minor stream coming from a spring crosses the trail. This is a good place to get water,

The Hare Trail takes you up a green and gentle valley to the Divide.

PHOTO BY LIZ THOMAS

as you are likely to not find another water source right on the trail.

In about 0.5 mile, you reach a broad, beautiful meadow several hundred yards away from the trail. This is a great place to camp and you can often spot grazing animals here. This camp is 2.0 miles and 800 feet of climbing from your car.

If you choose to continue, the Hare Trail will make a sharp left turn and head north up minor switchbacks, leaving the creek. As noted, there is no water on the Divide, so fill up and purify before leaving the creek.

From here, the climb becomes more gradual, opening into broad tundra. Ascend some minor switchbacks about 2.5 miles into your hike and you will intersect with a broad trail, the CDT. A sign indicates that you are on the Hare Trail, but does not say CDT. To the south, you can see Trail Creek and an open meadow. In total, the elevation gain to the Divide from your car is about 1,100 feet.

When you reach the Divide, turn left to take the CDT north to access the heart of the Sierra Madre Ridge. (This trail is also known as the Wyoming Trail No. 1101.)

The CDT in this section is relatively flat and forested.   PHOTO BY LIZ THOMAS

Although the trail and surrounding area appear flat here, you are walking right on top of the Divide. To your left is the Hahns Peak/Bears Ears Ranger District of Routt National Forest. To your right is the Mount Zirkel Wilderness. The trail rolls gently through conifer forest and wildflower-filled meadows. Breaks in the trees offer incredible views of Hahns Peak (10,839 feet) to the southwest and a valley with Manzanares Lake to the east.

After about 1.8 miles on the CDT, you climb to a high point at 10,188 feet. Descend switchbacks, losing about 200 feet over 0.4 mile, to a saddle. There is a signed intersection with the Manzanares Trail here. If the weather is good, this is a fine spot for a lunch break and to take in the views. Retrace your steps back to the trailhead, taking care to keep your eyes open for the signed intersection back to the Hare Trail.

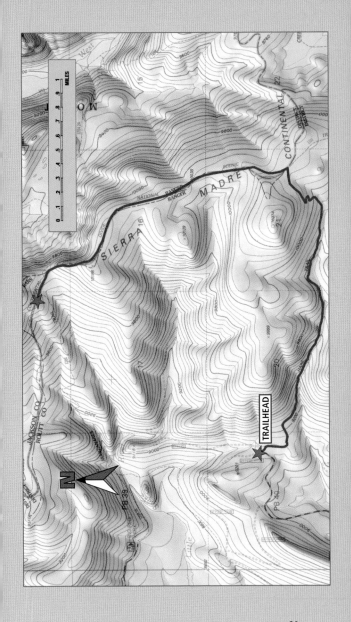

2. Lost Ranger Peak

MAPS	Trails Illustrated, Hahns Peak/ Steamboat Lake, Number 116 and Clark/Buffalo Pass, Number 117; Continental Divide Scenic Trail Map Book: Colorado, Bear Creek Survey, Maps 83–84, Segment 42; Guthook App Mile 1506.5 to 1497.1
ELEVATION GAIN	4,072 feet (with a 2,800-foot option)
RATING	Extreme (with moderate and difficult options), or as a moderate overnighter, or as an easy three-day trip
ROUND-TRIP DISTANCE	18.4 miles (with 6.0, 11.0 mile, and 12.5 mile options)
ROUND-TRIP TIME	12 hours, or as an overnighter, or as a three-day trip
NEAREST LANDMARK	Upper Three Island Lake Trailhead

COMMENT: Lost Ranger Peak is the highest peak on the CDT in the Mount Zirkel Wilderness—one of the original areas protected under the 1964 Wilderness Act. The Zirkels, as they are affectionately called, are home to 70 lakes, 15 peaks over 12,000 feet, and 36 miles of the CDT. On this hike to Lost Ranger Peak (which is just shy of 12,000 feet), you can ramble along rolling alpine tundra, observe fields of wildflowers, and walk in ancient forests of krummholz—crooked and twisted elfin trees that are stunted from exposure to wind and cold.

The route described here is a lollipop loop—a hike with a loop component (the candy part of the lollipop) and an out-and-back component (the stick part). The loop portion of the hike is formed by two trails that are used as the CDT. The two trails meet on the Divide. From this juncture, you can walk to and from the peak on the CDT—the out-and-back portion of the hike.

Krummholz are elfin trees that become twisted from living in harsh conditions, like at the top of mountains.   PHOTO BY LAWTON "DISCO" GRINTER

The trip to Lost Ranger Peak can be done as a big day trip, an overnighter, or as a three-day trip. If you are looking for a moderate trip, we suggest the hike to Three Island Lake (6.0 miles round-trip); or to North Lake (11.0 miles round-trip); or combining the two lakes into a loop that skips Lost Ranger Peak (difficult; 12.3-mile loop).

The large Seedhouse Campground is an ideal staging area for before or after your hike. Although Three Island Lake and North Lake would seemingly make good camping areas, please respect posted camping restrictions requiring that campers stay 0.25 mile from the lakes.

You will pass several streams, creeks, and lakes, but remember there is no water on the Divide (except for a seasonal stream 1.6 miles from Lost Ranger Peak), so carry sufficient amounts with you. The hike goes above treeline at times, so check the weather before you go and move to lower elevations if the weather turns.

Because the section of the CDT from the Three Island Lake Trailhead to the North Lake Trailhead is open to many uses, be aware of other users. Bikes should yield

Cairns mark the way to Lost Ranger Peak.   PHOTO BY LAWTON "DISCO" GRINTER

to hikers. Hikers should yield to horses. Motorized users should yield to all nonmotorized traffic.

GETTING THERE: The Seedhouse Trailhead can be accessed on good dirt roads in a two-wheel-drive vehicle. As the trailhead is relatively high, the road is open only during the summer. Check road conditions before starting.

From Steamboat Springs, take Colorado Highway 129 north for 20.0 miles, just past the town of Clark. Turn right on Seedhouse Road (also called County Road 60 or FS 400) and follow it for about 3.0 miles. Turn right on FS 443, passing the Seedhouse Campground loops. The Upper Three Island Lake Trailhead is on the north (left) side of the road.

THE ROUTE: Start at the Upper Three Island Trailhead and be sure to sign the register. (On some older maps, the Three Island Lake Trail is shown as the old CDT.) After a minor uphill section for 0.2 mile, at the intersection turn right on the Three Island Lake Trail No. 1163 toward Three

Island Lake, headed northeast. Ignore the spur trail. You will slowly ascend through aspen, which display brilliant colors in the fall. Continue upward on good trail, climbing through spruce, fir, and lodgepole pine. There are a few minor creek crossings.

After about 1.7 miles, you cross North Three Island Creek. Follow the creek east until you see a clearing near a distinctive feature called Lookout Rock. From here, you will have an excellent view of the South Fork of the Elk River Valley.

The terrain mellows as you reach Three Island Lake. Wilderness regulations do not permit camping near the lake. The hike to Three Island Lake is 3.0 miles, with 2,800 feet of elevation gain; an out-and-back hike to the lake can be a scenic and fun moderate trip.

If you choose to go onto the CDT, continue east past the northern edge of Three Island Lake. Follow the Three Island Lake Trail as it ascends moderately through less steep terrain. After about 0.5 mile, the waterway and the trail head south. Cross an outlet of Beaver Lake and continue south through sometimes swampy terrain. Continue gradually ascending. You will reach treeline at around 10,700 feet. In about 0.3 mile, you cross the waterway for the last time. Be sure to collect water here as there is no guaranteed water on the section along the physical Divide. About 0.25 mile later, turn right on what is marked on some maps as the old CDT south.

Follow the old CDT as it dips in and out of treeline. Here on the Divide, you may see some of the krummholz for which this area is famous. You will also roll along green hills with excellent views of the Zirkels. After 0.8 mile, you will see a trail on your right. This is the North Lake Trail (also known as the new CDT), which you can take to return to your car if you choose to do just the loop portion of the hike (about 11.5 miles). If you choose to continue on to Lone Ranger Peak, stay straight on the CDT south.

Open tundra walks offer spectacular views of the surrounding areas.

PHOTO BY LAWTON "DISCO" GRINTER

The trail descends to a low point after 1.2 miles, where you may find a seasonal creek. Get some water here before starting the final 1.6-mile ascent to the summit. Most of the climb is above treeline, although you may see krummholz. The trail is marked with cairns.

The CDT comes very close to the summit of Lost Ranger Peak. You can access the summit by leaving the trail and heading 0.15 mile east. When you are ready, retrace your steps by following the CDT north for 2.8 miles. When you reach the intersection with the North Lake Trail, turn left (west) onto the North Lake Trail/new CDT north.

Descend from the Divide. You will see a small pond to your right and soon you will cross an outlet of the pond. This may be the first water you cross on the trail since before you reached the Divide.

Continue to head west on the North Lake Trail, following a waterway to very near North Lake. Please follow camping restrictions in this area.

For the next 1.3 miles, the trail is less steep as it turns west and then northwest. From there, it follows a steep ridge northwest as the trail descends for 1.0 mile. You will come near a stream on your right and continue your descent, via switchbacks, for 1.1 miles until you reach the North Lake Trailhead near jeep trail #443. Turn right on the jeep trail and continue north for 0.6 mile on mild terrain. Cross the north fork of Three Island Creek and follow the creek at a distance for 0.8 mile until you reach the Upper Three Island Lake Trailhead—the same trailhead you started at many miles before.

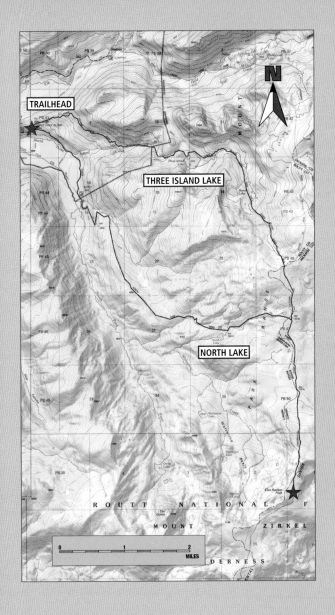

TRAILHEAD

THREE ISLAND LAKE

NORTH LAKE

N

ROUTT   NATIONAL   F

MOUNT   ZIRKEL

0   1   2
MILES

DERNESS

3. Parkview Mountain

MAPS	Trails Illustrated, Rand/Stillwater Pass, Number 115; Continental Divide Scenic Trail Map Book: Colorado, Bear Creek Survey, Segments 38–39, Map 74; Guthook App Mile 1415.7 to 1420.5
ELEVATION GAIN	2,913 feet (one-way)
RATING	Difficult, with difficult navigation
ROUND-TRIP DISTANCE	10 miles
ROUND-TRIP TIME	8 hours
NEAREST LANDMARK	Willow Creek Pass Parking Area

COMMENT: Parkview Mountain is one of the most iconic mountains on the CDT. For those walking the entire CDT southbound from Canada to Mexico, Parkview Mountain is the first time hikers reach 12,000 feet after traveling across miles of isolated northern Colorado. Yet, for dayhikers, Parkview Mountain is easily accessible and can be summitted in hours.

Parkview is one of the highest peaks in its area and thus offers hikers some of the best views along the CDT in northern Colorado. Hikers can view North Park, Rocky Mountain National Park, the Never Summer Range, and the Indian Peaks. At 12,396 feet, Parkview is the highest and most massive mountain in the Rabbit Ears Range. In fact, the building on the top of Parkview, erected in 1916, is the second-highest-elevation fire observatory ever built in the United States.

Like much of the CDT, this section of trail utilizes old roadbeds, jeep trails, new single-track, and cairn-to-cairn hiking. As a result of this, the navigation can sometimes be confusing. However, the trail is generally marked with

Parkview Mountain is a major landmark on the CDT, as this photo of the mountain taken from the CDT south of the mountain shows.

posts showing CDT markers at all intersections, so be observant and you can discover the true navigational adventure that makes the CDT such a wild trail. As you get closer to the mountain, the route is marked only with posts or cairns, which are not always easy to see. You may need binoculars to find your next post. As always, bring your map and compass and be prepared to use them.

Snow can accumulate on Parkview Mountain and stick until July. The mountain is especially susceptible to avalanches in the spring. Although mountaineers climb Parkview during the winter, it is not advised to use the route the CDT follows as it ascends an avalanche-prone basin east of the summit.

Be sure to bring plenty of water, especially if you are hiking the trail in late summer or early fall, as there is often no water along this hike.

GETTING THERE: From Granby, take Colorado 125 north for 24.4 miles to Willow Creek Pass. From Walden, take Colorado 125 south for 32.1 miles. The trailhead is just south of the pass, with parking on the east side of the road.

THE ROUTE: From the Willow Creek Pass parking lot, cross to the west side of the highway and follow signs to the CDT Trailhead (9,621 feet). Follow the footpath for 0.2 mile until

Follow the CDT along the spine of the massive Parkview Mountain for some of the best views in northern Colorado.

PHOTO BY JOHNNY "BIGFOOT" CARR

you reach a trail junction, at which point you bear right. Continue up a ridge using switchbacks for the next 0.5 mile until you reach a relative high point at 10,400 feet. From here, you may be able to see Little Haystack Mountain to the west.

Continue along the ridge for about a mile until you reach a junction with a dirt road. (Some maps show the CDT as continuing straight to Parkview Creek valley and then following the northwest spur ridge to the northern ridge of Parkview Mountain to the summit. This old route follows well-built cairns and includes some off-trail travel that is not described here.) *Instead of taking that path*, you should turn left to join the road here to stay on the new CDT, completed in 2012. Much of this trail was built by Rocky Mountain Youth Corps with funding provided by Great Outdoors Colorado and Colorado State Parks.

Walk the dirt road, heading southeast 0.2 mile, until you reach another intersection. It should have CDT posts indicating you should head straight and to the right at the junction (instead of making a sharp turn with the road). Continue on single-track for 0.3 mile until you reach another intersection, where you turn right.

Follow a dirt road for 1.0 mile. Turn left at a junction, which may not be signed, around 10,910 feet, heading slightly downhill towards a seasonal creek. Cross the creek and follow the ridge up above treeline. From here, you can follow cairns for 0.8 mile as the trail winds its way towards the summit.

The trail can be steep, and at times, the trail tread may disappear altogether. You will be able, however, to see posts dotting the way up the alpine tundra. Continue to climb steeply as the trail heads due south for 0.3 mile. Then it turns toward the southwest, following the ridge. Continue to follow cairns and stay high on the ridge. Due to the high altitude, the wildflower season is short—from late June

Climbing towards the summit on high tundra.

PHOTO BY STEVEN "TWINKLE" SHATTUCK

This gentle ridge of Parkview and Haystack Mountains is visible from the summit.

PHOTO BY JOHNNY "BIGFOOT" CARR

until early August—but you may be able to spot some short-growing species in this area.

When you reach the summit of Parkview Mountain, you can luxuriate in the ultimate reward: The view from the top looks out on the Flat Tops, the Gore Range, the Tenmile Range, the Collegiate Range, and the Front Range. For long-distance hikers, it is an excellent vantage point to review where you are going and where you have been.

There is a National Historic Lookout Register in the old lookout building atop the mountain. The building should be unlocked and can provide an excellent respite from the wind. Please refrain from adding more graffiti, including your name, to the building. To return to your car, retrace your steps, taking care not to mistake the route you took up for the "other CDT" that follows cairns along the northern ridge of Parkview.

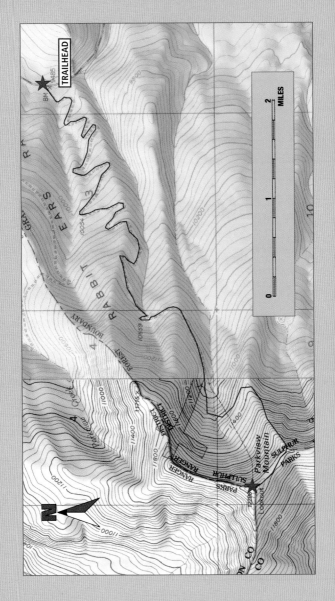

TRAILHEAD

N

MILES
0   1   2

4. Rocky Mountain National Park Loop

MAPS	Trails Illustrated, Rocky Mountain National Park, Number 200; Continental Divide Scenic Trail Map Book: Colorado, Bear Creek Survey, Segment 36, Maps 68–70; Guthook App Mile 1370.0 to 1392.1
ELEVATION GAIN	4,326 feet
RATING	Moderate overnighter (with moderate dayhike option)
ROUND-TRIP DISTANCE	25.3-mile loop (with a 10-mile out-and-back option to Granite Falls)
ROUND-TRIP TIME	All-day, overnight, or easy three-day trip
NEAREST LANDMARK	Grand Lake, CO

COMMENT: Twenty-eight miles of the Continental Divide Trail consists of a loop trail through Rocky Mountain National Park. Done as a long day-hike, as an overnight trip, or as a multi-day trip, this loop takes hikers through montane and subalpine life systems at elevations of 8,000 to 11,500 feet. The hike is an excellent way to explore the park's less traveled (and less crowded) west side. One-third of the hike is above treeline, rising above verdant valleys, twisting rivers, and glistening lakes—offering stunning views of the Continental Divide.

As it is a loop hike, hikers can do this route either clockwise or counterclockwise. Walked as a clockwise hike, the trail ascends to the Divide more gradually and hikers have access to more camping options before reaching timberline. West of the Divide, lodgepole pines dominate the lower elevations while aromatic Douglas, subalpine firs, and Engelmann spruce adorn higher points. Hikers have the

The trail is well defined through Rocky Mountain National Park.

PHOTO BY LANCE STACK

opportunity of walking along the Divide and looking down on some of the remaining glaciers in Rocky Mountain National Park.

In 2013, a lightning strike caused the Big Meadows Fire in the park and sections of the Rocky Mountain Loop were closed. They have since been reopened. This hike provides an excellent example of forest disturbance and succession.

At higher altitudes, snow patches may remain along the trail throughout the summer. Campsites are available just below treeline, giving hikers the opportunity to visit alpine areas in the morning and descend below treeline in the afternoon, when thunderstorms are more prevalent. If you see storm clouds or hear thunder, it is advisable to turn back and finish the hike on another day.

Designated campsites are numerous along the trails. A backcountry permit is required for overnight camping. Permits can be obtained from the Kawuneeche Visitor Center or by calling 970-627-3471, or the RMNP Backcountry Office, 970-586-2371. Please note that dogs are not allowed in Rocky Mountain National Park.

Although this hike is the official route of the CDT, signs may not always indicate "Continental Divide Trail," but

A hiker enjoys Granite Falls.

may show local trail names used within the park. Be sure to use this book and your map and compass to orient yourself on this loop.

GETTING THERE: *North Inlet Trailhead*: Take US 34 to the town of Grand Lake. Exit on US 278/West Portal Road and go 1.2 miles. Turn left onto County Road 663 and take it for 0.2 mile. The trailhead is north of town, near the filtration plant. Parking is available at the North Inlet Trailhead. For those walking the Rocky Mountain Loop clockwise, walk 300 feet east on County Road 663 and cross Tonahutu Creek. Continue 200 more feet to the Tonahutu Creek Trail, on your right.

THE ROUTE: For hikers going clockwise, start on the Tonahutu Creek Trail, which is accessed by walking 0.1 mile west on County Road 663. Follow the trail along Tonahutu Creek for 0.8 mile until you reach an intersection; turn right. After another 0.1 mile you will reach an intersection with the Kawuneeche Visitor Center Trail on your left. This trail connects to the Park Service Visitor Center 0.7 mile to the west. Stay on the Tonahutu Creek Trail heading north, which will take you up the eastern slopes of Green Mountain (10,313 feet). Watch for moose and elk in the several small meadows. After 1.7 miles, you will pass the first backcountry campsite, Paintbrush Camp. Shortly after, you will reach a signed junction indicating the Green Mountain Trail to the west and the Tonahutu Creek Trail to the north.

Ignore the Green Mountain Trail and follow the Tonahutu Creek Trail north as it ascends, skirting Big Meadow,

A peaceful meadow on the RMNP Loop.   PHOTO BY CDTC STAFF

the largest montane meadow in the Park. Tonahutu is the Arapaho word for "big meadows." Two miles into the hike, pass the ruins of an old cabin that belonged to an early homesteader. At a signed junction with the Onahu Creek Trail, continue east on the Tonahutu Trail as it ascends through a lodgepole pine forest and meadows, slowly following the Tonahutu Creek upstream. Many of the conifers in this area have died from the mountain pine beetle.

About a mile from the last trail junction you will reach Sunset Backcountry Campsite, and 0.5 mile later you will reach the Sunrise Backcountry Campsite on the east side of the meadow. Both of these camps make an excellent place to stay for those wishing to make the loop a three-day trip.

Soon you will walk through a part of the trail that burned in the Big Meadow Fire of 2013. Despite the burn, wildflowers abound in this area in summer. Watch for blowdowns—trees that have fallen across the trail. Be alert, also, for damaged trees angling across or in the direction of the trail; these can be quite dangerous, especially in windy conditions.

Approximately 5.0 miles into the hike, you will reach the Lower Granite Falls Backcountry Campsite and, shortly after, Granite Falls. These falls have three granite tiers. Soon after the falls, you will reach the Granite Falls Backcountry Campsite on the edge of a wet meadow.

Highlights of this hike include meadows and streams.

PHOTO BY LANCE STACK

As you continue on the trail, you will pass the Tonahutu Meadows and Tonahutu Group campsites (about 6.2 and 6.6 miles into the hike) and the Renegade Campsite (7.3 miles). Timberline Camp, located at 10,500 feet, is 7.5 miles into the hike and located right at treeline. These all make excellent options if you wish to make the hike a multi-day or overnight trip.

Shortly after these campsites, you will reach treeline below the summit of Sprague Mountain (12,713 feet). On the other side of the divide are Sprague Glacier and Rainbow Lake. Follow the Tonahutu Creek Trail/CDT as it heads southwest below Sprague Pass. The trail becomes a rocky, wildflower-filled alpine plateau, flattening out at Bighorn Flats, which offers impressive alpine views and great, easy walking.

Next you will travel along the eastern slopes of Gabletop Mountain (11,639 feet), Knobtop Mountain (12,331 feet), and Notchtop Mountain (10,129 feet) before approaching Ptarmigan Pass. Snow can linger here late into the season and a permanent snowfield sits on the northern bowl below Ptarmigan Point (12,363 feet—the bump just north of the pass). Ptarmigan Point is the westernmost summit along the glacier-carved wall of Odessa Gorge. From here, you will have impressive views of the most famous mountain in the park, Longs Peak (14,255 feet).

The path up to Tonahutu Ridge.

After about 12 miles and 2,000 feet of gained altitude into your trip, you will reach a three-way signed junction. If you continue west for 0.25 mile, you will reach the summit of Flattop Mountain (12,324 feet), a popular day-hike that most people ascend from the eastern slope. To continue on the CDT, turn right (south) onto the North Inlet Trail. Shortly after this junction you reach the Continental Divide—the high point of this trip, at 12,324 feet. From here, you have beautiful, unspoiled views of the basin to the west. Just on the other side of the divide, to the east, lies the Tyndall Glacier.

Descend south on the trail. Hallett Peak (12,713 feet) and Otis Peak (12,495 feet) loom to your east. Below Andrews Pass, the trail makes a sharp turn westward, following a series of switchbacks to take you below treeline. As you reenter the trees, you cross Hallett Creek. Shortly after, you will see a ranger patrol cabin south of the trail. Follow the creek, descending gradually until you reach another series of short switchbacks.

Approximately 4.5 miles from the intersection with Flattop Mountain—after the switchbacks—the trail veers northwest away from Hallett Creek to a signed intersection with the Lake Nanita Trail. For a side trip, you can head south on the Lake Nanita Trail for 0.25 mile to the North Inlet Falls. After you have visited the falls, return to

This hike stays on the less-crowded, western side of RMNP, but still gets views of the eastern side of the Park. PHOTO BY CDTC STAFF

the junction and continue to follow the North Inlet Trail, northwest, as it follows Inlet Creek.

After a short set of switchbacks, you will reach Porcupine Campsite, 6.75 miles from the North Inlet Trailhead. Cross a footbridge over Ptarmigan Creek shortly after and then pass the North Inlet Group Site and the Grouseberry Campsite. Gently descend along the creek to a footbridge over Big Pool, located 4.8 miles from the North Inlet Trailhead. Pass through a large meadow, popular for wildlife viewing, at 4.0 miles from the trailhead.

Walk along a north valley wall above the creek before reaching Twinberry Backcountry Camp, approximately 3.0 miles from the trailhead.

At 1.2 miles from the trailhead, you will reach Summerland Park—a mixed meadow and wooded area that is excellent for watching wildlife.

Follow the North Inlet Trail southwest until you reach the North Inlet Trailhead. You have successfully completed the Rocky Mountain National Park loop on the CDT!

GRANITE FALLS

TRAILHEAD

5. Arapahoe Bay to Knight Ridge

MAPS	Trails Illustrated, Rocky Mountain National Park, Number 200; Continental Divide Scenic Trail Map Book: Colorado, Bear Creek Survey, Map 66, Segment 35; Guthook App Mile 1365 to 1355.5
ELEVATION GAIN	1,647 feet
RATING	Easy–moderate (or as a family-friendly overnighter
ONE-WAY TRIP DISTANCE	9.8 miles with camping at 1.6 miles and 2.2 miles in
ONE-WAY TRIP TIME	5 hours
NEAREST LANDMARK	Green Ridge Campground, Roaring Fork Campground

COMMENT: This easily accessible, beautiful lake walk is a great introduction to hiking the CDT and is ideal for folks who want a gentler hike. The CDT throughout this section is relatively flat, with minor elevation gain, so it is a good option for families. There are numerous opportunities for swimming and fishing, making this hike a great opportunity for kids to explore nature.

For hikers who want to turn the Knight Ridge experience into an overnight trip, there are several campsites along the way and there are campgrounds at the beginning and end of the hike. In Rocky Mountain National Park (Green Ridge Campground to Twin Creek), camping is allowed only in designated sites and permits are required. We recommend getting one in advance as many of these campgrounds fill up quickly. Permits can be obtained from the Kawuneeche Visitor Center, or by calling 970-627-3472, or the RMNP Backcountry Office, 970-586-2371.

After Twin Creek, the hike crosses into Arapaho National Forest. The last four miles of the hike go through the

A bald eagle sits high on a branch near Columbine Bay just south of Grand Lake.
PHOTO BY JOHNNY "BIGFOOT" CARR

Indian Peaks Wilderness. A permit is also required here for overnight camping. Call the Sulphur Ranger District at 970-887-4100 for details.

The first half of the trip travels through Rocky Mountain National Park and the second through Arapaho National Forest and the Indian Peaks Wilderness (part of Arapaho National Forest). RMNP does not allow dogs or bicycles and the Indian Peaks Wilderness prohibits bicycles.

The route described below is a one-way trip that will require a car shuttle—with one car at the northern East Shore Dam Trailhead and another at the Roaring Fork Trailhead. Alternately, you can choose to hike in as far as you would like and make the trip an out-and-back. If you are coming from Granby, we suggest dropping off your first car at the Roaring Fork Trailhead and driving the second car to the Green Ridge Campground.

Lake Granby.   PHOTO BY JOHNNY "BIGFOOT" CARR

GETTING THERE: From Granby, take US Highway 34 northwest for 12 miles. A brown recreation sign will indicate where to turn right (east) on County Road 66 (also known as Forest Road 274) towards Green Ridge. Follow County Road 66 for 1.0 mile, passing a campground and picnic area, until you cross a bridge over the lake outlet. Continue for another 0.2 mile until you reach the Green Ridge Campground. Turn north (left) to follow County Road 66 between the campground loops until you reach the shore of Shadow Mountain Lake. Park along the road on the right. The East Shore Dam Trailhead holds about 12 cars. Toilets are available at the nearby campgrounds. The Arapaho National Forest Recreation area requires a $5 parking fee or a valid recreation pass.

To get to the Roaring Fork Trailhead: From Granby, take US Highway 34 northwest for 9.1 miles. Turn right on County Road 6 and stay on it for 8.8 miles as it skirts the southern lakeshore. Turn left on County Road 637 and drive north through the Arapaho Bay Campground for 0.9 mile. Park at the Roaring Fork/Knight Ridge/CDT Trailhead.

THE ROUTE: From your parking spot at the East Shore Dam Trailhead, walk the road over Shadow Mountain Dam, which separates Shadow Mountain Lake from the Colorado River. Walk northeast along the road for 0.1 mile, passing the dam and coming to a place where the wide road makes a sharp turn. At the point of the turn, turn left to intersect with the East Shore Trail, which you will find about 50 feet later. Turn right on the East Shore Trail (which is marked on some maps as the CDT). Follow the East Shore Trail southwest for 0.3 mile, on mostly flat (although sometimes muddy) terrain and cross over Ranger Creek.

Follow the trail south for 0.1 mile until you reach an intersection. Although on some maps it shows that the CDT is to the left, stay straight, heading west on a path deeper into the woods, through mostly flat, grassy terrain. After 0.4 mile, you will intersect the CDT, also known in this area as the Ranger Meadows Trail.

Turn right (south) on the CDT, and walk through meadows with conifer forest to your left. About 0.5 mile later, ignore a trail that joins from the right and ignore another trail that joins from the right 0.2 mile later. (These trails are also marked on some maps as the CDT.)

Soon you will cross Pole Creek, which starts near Mount Bryant and feeds into the Colorado River nearby. Follow the CDT as it parallels the Colorado River to Columbine Bay. Here the trail goes through the Columbine Bay Campground. If you want to turn your trip into an overnighter, this is a good place to stay.

Cross over Columbine Creek and follow the river shore for 0.6 mile, where you will reach the Grand Bay Campground. This is another good overnight option. At 0.6 mile farther, cross over an unnamed creek. The CDT follows the river shore south to Grand Bay, where it crosses over Twin Creek on a log footbridge.

Near a Forest Service cabin at Grand Bay, the CDT breaks from the river shore and heads directly south. You will gradually climb Knight Ridge through aspen stands before

Wildflowers covered in raindrops after a storm near Monarch Lake.

PHOTO BY JOHNNY "BIGFOOT" CARR

the trail levels out. This section of the CDT is called the Knight Ridge Trail on some maps.

After 2.2 miles along Knight Ridge, you will reach a small pond on your left—a good place for a lunch break. From here, the trail switchbacks down for 1.3 miles towards the shore of Lake Granby at MacDonald Cove. (This path is steeper than the one up Knight Ridge). Toward the bottom of the ridge, there are few trees on the slope and you should have a great view of the lake.

Follow the trail along the eastern lake shore through lodgepole pine for another 1.2 miles, until you approach some beaver ponds and cross the Roaring Fork Arapaho Creek on a wooden bridge. Shortly after, you will reach the Roaring Fork Trailhead, where you may have left a vehicle. The Arapaho Bay Moraine Campground is 0.4 mile down the road, and can be a good place to rest after finishing your hike and before retrieving your other vehicle from the Shadow Mountain Dam Trailhead where you started your hike.

Fallen trees

In 2011, a microburst windstorm brought down many trees, 80 percent of which were already dead from attacks by the mountain pine beetle. In 2015, the US Forest Service, Continental Divide Trail Coalition volunteers, and partner organizations removed 800 fallen trees—cross-cutting and removing most of the trees by hand. Thanks to the volunteers, this beautiful section is accessible once again and offers panoramic views of the lakes and of RMNP.

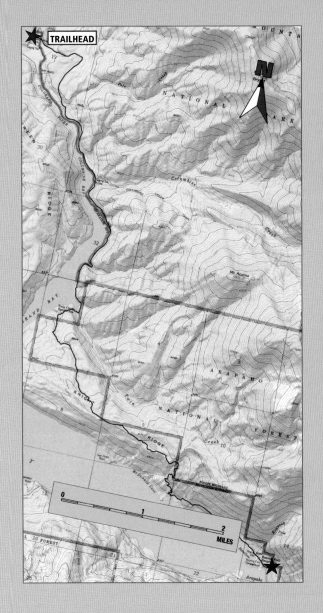

6. Rollins and Rogers Passes and James Peak

MAPS	Trails Illustrated, Winter Park/ Central City/Rollins Pass, Number 103; Continental Divide Scenic Trail Map Book: Colorado, Bear Creek Survey, Segment 33, Maps 61–62; Guthook App Mile 1370.0 to 1392.1
ELEVATION GAIN	2,815 feet (one-way)
RATING	Difficult
ROUND-TRIP DISTANCE	13.2 miles round-trip
ROUND-TRIP TIME	8 hours (4 hours one-way)
NEAREST LANDMARK	Rollins Pass

COMMENT: Although just 50 miles west of Denver, many long-distance hikers call James Peak and its surrounding area the "most magical part of the entire CDT." This 13,294-foot peak is so impressive that an entire wilderness is named after it. The alpine traverse and walk up to James Peak gives hikers top-of-the-world exposure and big views into Rocky Mountain National Park and the James Peak Wilderness, which was designated by Congress in 2001. History buffs will enjoy visiting two passes that are important in Colorado's history: Rollins Pass and Rogers Pass.

James Peak is named after Dr. Edwin James, a botanist for Major Stephen Long's 1820 exploration of Colorado. Dr. James was also the first person to climb Pikes Peak. Gilpin, Clear Creek, and Grand Counties share James Peak and it serves as a boundary marker separating the counties.

As this hike starts right on the Divide, at almost 12,000 feet, the elevation gain over the course of the hike is relatively manageable in spite of the high elevation of James Peak. Some of the hike lacks trail and requires you to follow

A thru-hiker enjoys the views from the tundra walk just north of James Peak.

PHOTO BY JOHNNY "BIGFOOT" CARR

posts and cairns, but as you are above treeline, there is a clear line of sight to where you need to go.

Many hikers visit Rogers Pass every summer, usually opting to take the crowded Rogers Pass Trail from the packed East Portal Trailhead. By starting your hike at Rollins Pass, you can experience more high country hiking with fewer people. However, for those without four-wheel-drive, starting at the East Portal Trailhead near Moffat Tunnel and following the Rogers Pass Trail up Boulder Creek is a good way to access James Peak and enjoy a pleasant overnight trip.

This hike starts right on the Continental Divide at Rollins Pass (11,676 feet). Rollins Pass was frequently used by Native Americans, and in 1862 James Rollins created a toll road over the Divide, giving the pass its current name. In the 19th century, the road was used to drive cows between the Front Range and Middle Park.

By 1903, the pass was used by trains traveling between Denver and Salt Lake City. Graded at 4 percent, the Denver, Northwestern, and Pacific Railway route over Rollins Pass was one of the steepest non-cog railways ever built. Trains crossed the Divide at Rollins Pass until 1928, when Moffat Tunnel was constructed. Rollins Pass was once home to the historic town of Corona, which housed train workers who were employed to keep snow off the tracks. Now, despite many hikers' deepest wishes, the grand restaurant and hotel are gone, and there is nothing left of the town.

For those walking the CDT southbound from Canada to Mexico, James Peak marks the first time hikers reach a 13,000-foot peak. Many hikers, even the fit and expe-

Wildflowers below a post marking the trail.

PHOTO BY JOHNNY "BIGFOOT" CARR

rienced, have some difficulty breathing at altitude. Be sure to drink plenty of water, take your trip slowly, and monitor for headaches or other symptoms of altitude sickness. Be aware that snow can linger until July or August and snowy slopes can be quite steep in parts of this hike.

GETTING THERE: From Winter Park, take US Highway 40 one mile east to County Road 80/Corona Pass Road/Forest Road 149, slightly east of the base of the Winter Ski Park Area. Before heading farther, note that this road is closed during the winter. It is best suited for four-wheel-drive and high clearance vehicles, and many skilled drivers in two-wheel-drive and all-wheel-terrain station wagons have not been able to make it all the way to Rollins Pass, especially after it rains. It is best to call the ranger district to ask about road conditions before heading to the pass. As the route is at a high altitude and not often plowed, think twice about taking the road early in the season. If you choose to continue, turn left onto County Road 80 (Forest Road 149) and follow it for 15 miles, ascending gradually along the old railroad bed to the Divide and Rollins Pass. Note that you cannot take your car to the western side of the Divide due to the collapsed Needle's Eye Tunnel. Be prepared to return the way you came. The parking lot at Rollins Pass has room for 15 cars.

THE ROUTE: From Rollins Pass, walk on the dirt Corona Pass Road/CR 80/FS 149 south, ignoring Road 501 on your left.

July is peak wildflower season for the area around Rollins Pass to James Peak.

After 0.5 mile, you will see trail/two-track on the east (left) side of the road. Follow this trail, climbing 400 feet over the next mile to a high point near a radio beacon. While it may look like the trail splits many times, ultimately, all paths lead to the same destination. (In fact, there is another trail that starts right at Rollins Pass, but it can be easy to miss, which is why we included the short road walk). If the path disappears, stay towards the western part of the Divide.

For the next 2.0 miles, stay along the ridge, which is the actual Continental Divide. There are minor undulations, but the trail generally sticks around 12,000 feet. The trail tread disappears at times, but CDT posts and cairns mark the route. The trail stays above treeline, so you should have a great line of sight for spotting posts. There are some large rocks in this area, but the route is generally not steep. Be gentle as you walk through this area as the vegetation can be sensitive and has a short growing season.

To the east are views of the James Peak Wilderness and numerous high lakes and tarns (glacier-formed lakes)—some of which may hold ice. Climb to a high point at 12,251 feet, where you will see the Rogers Pass Trail below you to the west (your right).

At 4.9 miles from Rollins Pass, you will see a trail join the CDT from the west (right). Ignore this trail and continue straight for a mile as you descend to Rogers Pass (11,949 feet), ignoring another wide trail that joins from the west (right).

About 0.2 mile after the intersection with the wide trail, make a slight right, leaving the wide trail and entering single-track trail. After 0.1 mile, you will reach Rogers Pass at a four-way intersection of trails. The Rogers Pass Trail N93 goes east–west. To the east, the trail travels near Heart Lake, descending along South Boulder Creek. Stay straight (south) to continue on the CDT.

Continue on the west side of the Continental Divide, heading south for 0.5 mile. On the other side of the Divide is Haystack Mountain. You will be walking on a steep ridge, so take care in this area, especially early in the season when snow may remain. After 0.2 mile, the trail turns left (east) along the Ute Trail and crosses over the Divide. Now on the eastern side of the Divide, you will find the slope less steep. Note that as you are at almost 13,000 feet, snow can stick here late into the season.

Pay special attention for an intersection with a narrow trail heading south (right) at 1.3 miles from Rogers Pass. Turn right onto this trail and ascend as it heads slightly east before you hit switchbacks 0.1 mile later. Follow the switchbacks along the northern face of James Peak for 0.5 mile until you reach the rocky summit.

From the summit, you can see Fraser to the north-northwest, Rocky Mountain National Park and Longs Peak to the north-northeast, and the Winter Park and Mary Jane Ski Areas to the northwest. The view to the south is the most impressive, though—the Continental Divide dotted with four other 13,000 foot peaks: Mt. Bancroft (13,250 feet) connected by a narrow ridge to the south; Parry Peak (13,391 feet) to the southwest; Mt. Eva (13,130 feet); and Mt. Flora (13,132 feet).

Retrace your steps to return to the parking lot.

James Peak Protection Area

To your west (right) is the James Peak Protection Area, with views of the Rollins Pass Road and Riflesight Notch. Although a "protection area" does not receive full wilderness status and protections from the Forest Service, mining, timber cutting, and building new roads are prohibited.

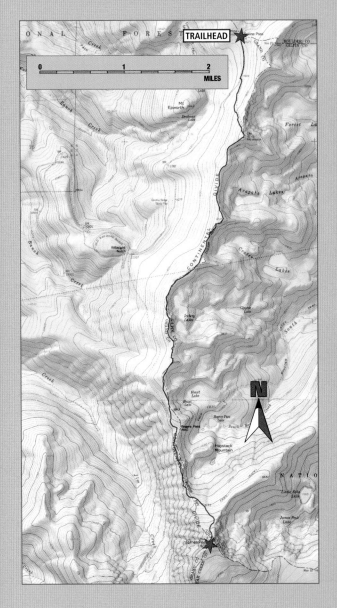

7. Berthoud Pass to Stanley Mountain

MAPS	Trails Illustrated, Winter Park/Central City/Rollins Pass, Number 103; Continental Divide Scenic Trail Map Book: Colorado, Bear Creek Survey, Maps 59–60, Segments 31–32; Guthook App Mile 1313.5 to 1309.8
ELEVATION GAIN	1,594 feet
RATING	Easy
ROUND-TRIP DISTANCE	6.9 miles
ROUND-TRIP TIME	4.5 hours
NEAREST LANDMARK	Berthoud Pass Parking Area

COMMENT: Berthoud Pass is named for Edward L. Berthoud, who "discovered" the pass in 1861, along with mountain man Jim Bridger. As a surveyor, Berthoud was searching for a low-grade railroad passage over the Divide. Deeming Berthoud Pass too steep for heavy machinery, it was used instead as a wagon road. In addition to his surveying, Berthoud served in the Union Army during the Civil War. Later he was elected mayor of Golden and then into the Colorado legislature. Berthoud also served as the Colorado territorial librarian, the Colorado state historian, and the first registrar of the Colorado School of Mines.

In 1937, the Berthoud Pass Ski Area opened. Some people claim that it was the first commercial ski resort in Colorado. Due to financial problems, the ski area closed in 2002 and its lodge was demolished in 2008. However, Berthoud Pass continues to attract winter backcountry enthusiasts—due to its steep terrain, easy access from the Front Range, and an average of 500 inches of snow annually.

Two hikers celebrate making it to the CDT kiosk at Berthoud Pass.

The hike described here starts from the Berthoud Pass parking lot, travels to the southwest, and cuts up and along the western slopes toward the Continental Divide. After the trail clears treeline, it enters the tundra zone. The trail continues its somewhat level grade until it reaches a small climb up switchbacks. It then enters the Vasquez Peak Wilderness. After a scenic ridge walk, you can scramble up Stanley Peak just off the CDT. This hike can be done as an out-and-back or you can choose to set up a car shuttle.

If you opt for a one-way trip, follow the CDT/Mt. Nystrom Trail south for another 2.0 miles to the intersection with the Henderson Spur Trail on the left. From there, it is another 0.9 mile to the Butler Creek Trailhead and parking area. Cars can access the trailhead from the Henderson Mine Road off of US 40, 5.8 miles west of Berthoud Pass. Proceed 1.8 miles and take the right fork onto Forest Service Road 202 for 0.5 mile. Parking is available along the road.

The route is well graded and well defined for the most part and is a great option for families. The trail winds in and out of conifers and onto smooth, bald mountaintops alternating with craggy terrain, rocky knolls, and wild-

The switchbacks up to Stanley Mountain.   PHOTO BY PETER "CZECH" SUSTR

flower patches. It offers views into Winter Park and the Front Range. In 2009, the warming hut, which also houses pit toilet facilities, was dedicated at the Pass. The developments and interpretive signs were part of a large statewide Great Outdoors Colorado grant to develop the Continental Divide Trail around Colorado. Much of the CDT on both sides of the highway was constructed and reconstructed at that time, using a combination of CDT volunteers and Rocky Mountain Youth Corps members. The highly visible monument to the Continental Divide Trail is a great place for simply taking in the amazing beauty of the Continental Divide itself.

GETTING THERE: From Denver, take Interstate 70 west to Exit 232/Empire/US 40 west and continue on US 40 for 15.1 miles to the top of Berthoud Pass (11,307 feet) at mile marker 243. From Winter Park or Fraser, take US 40 east for 45 miles to Berthoud Pass. Ample parking near the Berthoud Pass Trailhead, formerly the Berthoud Pass Ski Area, is available on the east side of US 40.

A walk through lush green meadows surrounded by high peaks.

THE ROUTE: From the Berthoud Pass parking lot, carefully cross US 40 to its west side and walk southwest for 0.1 mile along a well-defined path. The CDT departs right from US 40, up an embankment, and past a locked gate used to keep motorized vehicles off the trail. The trail ascends steeply through conifers and cascading meadows along the western slope of the Continental Divide. Keep an eye out for grouse and snowshoe hares in this subalpine zone. After 0.85 mile, the trail clears treeline and enters the tundra zone.

Continue on level trail onto a thin, narrow ridge on a flat, rocky plateau. After 0.4 mile of contouring (staying at relatively the same elevation as you traverse around the mountain), follow switchbacks to open tundra. In early summer, tundra flowers accent the landscape. You may also admire the views to the north into the Winter Park/Fraser Basin.

After a gentle climb up a ridge, you will reach the Vasquez Peak Wilderness boundary (12,390 feet).

Continuing around the ridge, the CDT aligns itself southwest, staying in the tundra zone. While the elevation stays

The Vasquez Peak Wilderness boundary.

PHOTO BY PETER "CZECH" SUSTR

relatively constant, you travel gently over three hills, which drain into three different basins. Look below for signs of elk and moose.

After 1.65 miles from the wilderness sign, the trail climbs gradually and Stanley Peak (12,521 feet) comes into view. An unassuming summit, Stanley Peak appears to be a rock pile on the left. Nonetheless, after a short scramble to the summit, you will encounter a steep drop on the south and west

side looking down into Butler Gulch. From the summit, you will have views of the impressive Vasquez Peak (12,947 feet) to the west. Retrace your steps to return to the Berthoud Pass parking area.

Wildflowers on the ridge up to Stanley Mountain.

PHOTO BY PETER "CZECH" SUSTR

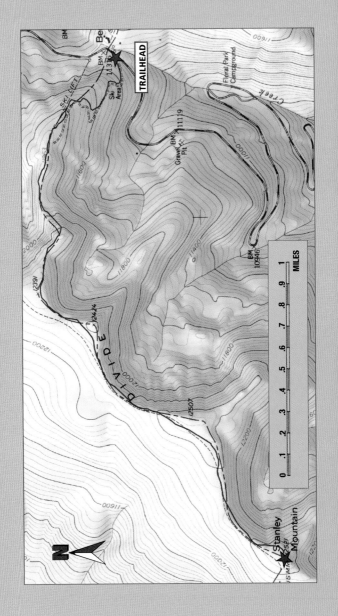

TRAILHEAD

BM
13

BM

Be

SKI LIFT

Ski
Area

Floral Park
Campground

Creek

Gravel BM 11119
Pit

BM
10946

11600

11800

2000

2391

DIVIDE

11800

11400

12000

12507

12200

12200

11900

Stanley
Mountain
12521

12000

N

MILES

0   .1   .2   .3   .4   .5   .6   .7   .8   .9   1

8. Herman Gulch

MAPS	Trails Illustrated, Idaho Springs/ Loveland Pass, Number 104; Continental Divide Scenic Trail Map Book: Colorado, Bear Creek Survey, Maps 57–58, Segment 31; Guthook App Mile 1292.9 to 1295.8
ELEVATION GAIN	800 feet (1,919 feet round-trip to Herman Lake)
RATING	Family friendly, (with easy-moderate option)
ROUND-TRIP DISTANCE	3 miles (Herman Lake 7.5 miles)
ROUND-TRIP TIME	2 hours (6 hours)
NEAREST LANDMARK	Herman Gulch Parking Area

COMMENT: Although only 45 minutes from Denver and a mere 1.5-mile hike, Herman Gulch is one of the best places for wildflower viewing on the entire CDT. The best time to see colorful wildflowers in bloom is mid- to late-July. The hike is also a popular snowshoeing route in winter, due to its accessibility and protection from the wind.

Summer hikers will be treated to a dazzling display of columbine, paintbrush, fairy trumpet flowers, kings crown, elephant flowers, assorted bell flowers, fireweed, forget-me-nots, alpine sunflowers, and moss campion. Due to the diversity of species of wildflowers along the trail, plant enthusiasts refer to the trail as a "100 wildflower" or "century" hike. Plan your trip schedule to account for extra time for wildflower photography.

A gulch by definition is a deep V-shaped valley formed by erosion. Herman Gulch was formed by Herman Creek, which eventually flows south-southeast to Clear Creek. You can tell when Herman Gulch ends when the trail starts ascending switchbacks and becomes steeper, and you reenter the woods. The beauty of this hike is that you don't have

The picturesque Herman Gulch trail.

to walk to Herman Lake or even the end of the gulch to enjoy the beauty of the area. At any time, just turn around and re-trace your steps back to the trailhead.

If you hike the entire distance of Herman Gulch and opt to continue on to Herman Lake, you will be rewarded with grand views of the open tundra and the valley below the Continental Divide. The hike provides abundant wildlife viewing opportunities, including the possibility of seeing moose, elk, bighorn sheep, and mountain goats.

This trip is perfect for families with small children and can be treated as an out-and-back hike for any distance. The trail is completely within the Clear Creek Ranger District of Arapaho National Forest.

In early spring, trail conditions may be muddy and mixed with well-worn packed-down snow and clear trail. Snow patches may remain along the trail throughout the summer. Be aware that the trailhead starts above 10,000 feet; make sure you are well acclimated before starting. Parts of the trail are above treeline, so plan to start the hike early, as afternoon thunderstorms are common in this area during the summer. If you see storm clouds or hear thunder, it is advisable to turn back and finish the hike on another day.

A dayhiker descends from Herman Lake.   PHOTO BY LIZ THOMAS

During peak season, in July, this hike is quite popular. Plan to get to the trailhead early as the parking lot can fill. Pit toilet facilities are available at the trailhead. A kiosk there has information about the Continental Divide Trail.

GETTING THERE: From Denver, take Interstate 70 west to Exit 218. Take a right at the off-ramp and stay on the north side of the interstate. The parking area and trailhead will be immediately visible to your right along a dirt road. Ample parking is available.

THE ROUTE: From the Herman Gulch parking lot, follow signs to the CDT Trailhead (10,375 feet). The CDT north, also called the Herman Gulch Trail #98, starts on a wide old sawmill road. You will travel northeast through a mixed aspen and fir forest for 0.25 mile before an obvious T intersection with the Watrous Gulch Trail #95 and the Bard Creek Trail. Turn left towards Herman Lake.

From here, climb a steep but relatively short hill until the CDT reaches the beautiful cascading Herman Creek. This part is the steepest and hardest climb of this trip. From here, you will ascend along the creek on wide, rocky tread. This section stays in heavy forest and is well shaded. (In spring and early summer, this section can be completely iced over from all the traffic it receives, so we suggest bringing traction devices for your shoes if you're hiking this section before June 15.)

After approximately 1.0 mile of moderate climbing, you will reach a long meadow, known as Lower Herman Gulch. In early summer, this area is strewn with wildflowers. The eastern slopes of Pettingell Peak (13,553 feet) and Hagar Mountain (13,195 feet) are visible to the west. The northern slopes of Mt. Bethel (12,705 feet) are visible to the south.

For the next mile, the trail becomes mellower, gradually climbing through open areas and meadows. Moose can be spotted in the willows along Herman Creek. You may be able to watch herds of elk grazing along the grassy slopes of Mt. Bethel to the south. Moose can be dangerous animals; don't try to approach them.

The wildflower-filled meadows near Herman Lake.   PHOTO BY LIZ THOMAS

The Herman Lake Trail seen from a hill above. PHOTO BY LIZ THOMAS

Walk as far or as little as you like to enjoy the beauty of this unique area. When you reenter the woods and the trail becomes steep again, you will know you are leaving the gulch and beginning the climb towards Herman Lake. If you choose to turn around at this point, retrace your steps back to the trailhead.

If you find yourself at the end of upper Herman Gulch and choose to continue on to Herman Lake, follow the CDT north as it enters the woods. The trail climbs steeply, ascending steadily above the gulch until you reach treeline approximately 2.5 miles from the trailhead. Shortly after, in an alpine area with open tundra flats, you will reach a signed intersection. Stay left, turning off the CDT, and follow the sign to Herman Lake. The CDT and Jones Pass goes up and switchbacks to your right.

From here, the terrain becomes gentler. As you near Herman Lake, the trail may become fainter, but you can follow obvious rock cairns to the lake. Watch for bighorn sheep and mountain goats grazing in this area. Subalpine flowers—smaller and lower-lying than those in Herman Gulch—line the trail and fill the rocky fields around you.

After 1.25 miles, you will reach the icy waters of the glacial Herman Lake. The steep wall of Pettingell Peak is visible along the eastern and northern shore. Hikers can enjoy an exceptional view of the lake and a panorama of the basin and upper gulch by climbing over a knoll along the lake's east shore. The CDT continues north via switchbacks to the west of Herman Lake. Retrace your steps to return to the parking lot.

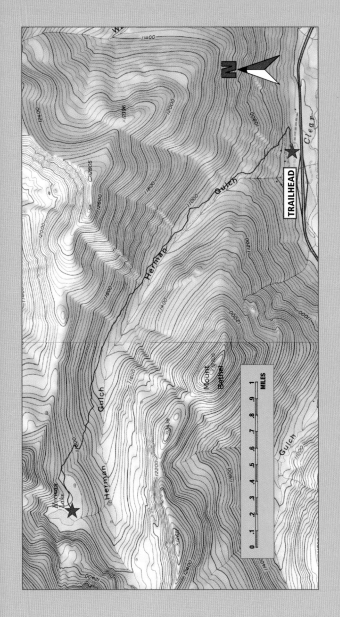

TRAILHEAD

MILES

0 .1 .2 .3 .4 .5 .6 .7 .8 .9 1

9. Argentine Pass to Mount Edwards

MAPS	Trails Illustrated, Idaho Springs/Loveland Pass, Number 104; Continental Divide Scenic Trail Map Book: Colorado, Bear Creek Survey, Map 56, Segment 29; Guthook App Mile 1279.9 to 1280.8
ELEVATION GAIN	3,051 feet
RATING	Difficult
ROUND-TRIP DISTANCE	7.1 miles
ROUND-TRIP TIME	6 hours
NEAREST LANDMARK	Argentine Pass Trailhead

COMMENT: If you're looking for a big view, and a short and stout hike that is close to the metro area, most locals will direct you to Grays and Torreys Peaks—among the two most climbed 14ers in Colorado. Grays Peak, at 14,270 feet, is the highest point on the CDT, and is among the most visited areas of the whole trail.

If you'd like all the pleasure of Grays and Torreys, but with fewer crowds, hop on the CDT from Argentine Pass to the near-14er, Mount Edwards. This hike is just a few miles south of those two famous 14ers, and offers similar views, a big workout, and the grandeur of the Divide—all close to the Denver metro area.

This hike will take you on a beautiful, newly constructed trail that bobs along the spine of the Divide. To the south, trail builders are working to connect this section all the way to Breckenridge, but on this hike you will be on well-maintained trail and an easy-to-navigate ridge the whole way. Be sure to check local conditions before you go as the hike is at a high altitude where snow

Jerry Brown looking from Argentine Peak at the CDT.

PHOTO BY TERESA MARTINEZ

can linger for a long time and avalanche danger in the spring is very high.

This ridge and general area see many hikers every summer and it's important to pack out all trash. Try to refrain from non-liquid bathroom breaks while on the ridge (or use a Wag Bag to carry it out), as human waste takes a very long time to biodegrade at this altitude and in this rocky terrain. As with all hikes above treeline on the CDT and in Colorado, be wary of afternoon thunderstorms and always check the weather before you go.

GETTING THERE: From Denver, take Interstate 70 west until you reach US 6 at Exit 216 with signs to the Loveland Pass Ski Area. Continue up US 6 west for 7.5 miles, going over Loveland Pass and down towards the Arapahoe Basin Ski Area. Continue south until you reach the northern outskirts of Keystone, which is about 5.0 miles from the Arapahoe Basin Ski Area. Turn left on Keystone Road, and immediately turn left onto Gondola Road and travel 0.3 mile. Turn right onto Montezuma Road and follow it for 4.3 miles as it heads west along the river. Then turn right on County Road 260 and follow it for 4.8 miles. At this point, the road will be closed with a locked gate. The Argentine Pass Trailhead parking area is along the road near this gate. There are pit toilets available.

THE ROUTE: From the Argentine Pass Trailhead parking area, walk north along the road for 0.1 mile and go through a closed gate indicating the road is closed to motorized vehicles. You will pass Shoe Basin Mine to your right (east) before turning onto single-track to your right (east) about 0.4 mile after the gate.

Head up steep trail, quickly ascending the western flanks of Argentine Peak. At 0.2 mile after you turn onto single-track, you will cross a creek. The trail continues southeast before making a sharp turn to your left (north). You will pass the same creek you crossed earlier. Be sure to get water here as it may be the last water you will see on the hike.

Continue contouring up the flank of Argentine Peak, generally heading north above Horseshoe Basin. Across the Basin, you will see Ruby Mountain (13,277 feet). Below you in the Basin is a jeep road providing access to numerous mines. To your direct south is Decatur Mountain (12,890 feet). The south side of Grays Peak (14,270 feet) is visible to the northwest. Directly to the north is your destination: Mount Edwards (13,850 feet).

After a short but steady climb, you will reach Argentine Pass at 13,484 feet. After you crest onto Argentine Pass, the CDT is routed right onto the Divide. Follow the CDT as it winds generally northwest towards Mount Edwards along the ridge. Mountain goats are numerous in this area and generally unafraid of humans. As with all wild animals, keep your distance and do not feed them.

After a little more than 1.0 mile from Argentine Pass, you will reach the summit of Mount Edwards (13,850 feet). Grays Peak is directly to the west on less defined trail. Mount Edwards tends to attract fewer people, so you can enjoy the grandeur of your summit without too much distraction. Retrace your steps to return to your car.

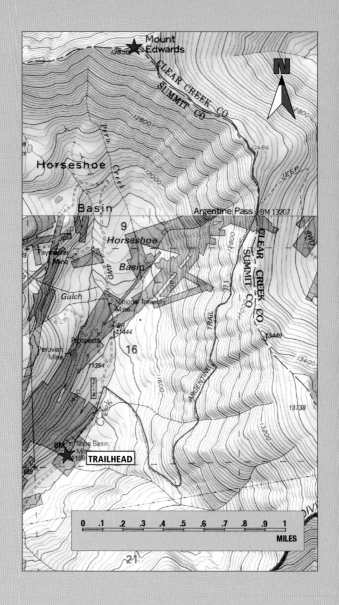

10. Tenmile Range

MAPS	Trails Illustrated, Vail/Frisco/Dillon, Number 108; Continental Divide Scenic Trail Map Book: Colorado, Bear Creek Survey, Maps 51–52, Segments 27–28; Guthook App Mile 1125.3 to 1237.7
ELEVATION GAIN	3,474 feet (one-way)
RATING	Difficult, or as an easy overnighter
ONE-WAY DISTANCE	11.5 miles
ONE-WAY TRIP TIME	8 hours
NEAREST LANDMARK	Breckenridge or Copper Mountain

COMMENT: If you're hankering for a one-way dayhike during your mountain summer vacation, but don't want to arrange for a shuttle, there is no better place to go than the Tenmile Range. A close drive from Denver with plenty of mountain town amenities nearby, the Tenmile Range gives hikers a sense of wilderness, a workout, and awesome views without difficult logistics and planning. The Summit Stage bus provides free rides 365 days a year, 19 hours a day between downtown Breckenridge, the Goldhill Trailhead, and Copper Mountain.

The climb to the Divide takes you past 1.7 billion-year-old basement rocks before traversing the crest, which looms over two well-visited mountain valleys. Tourists, however, are rarely afforded the views offered by the Tenmile Range Traverse. Taken from either direction, this hike starts in town and is well suited for folks enjoying mountain towns without a car or those who want to minimize drive time.

When hiked from Copper Mountain, the climb on this hike is gentler than if you start at the Goldhill Trailhead. Also, the plentiful streams along the east side of the Divide provide numerous opportunities to refill water bottles emptied on the climb up the crest. Moreover, ending a day's

A hiker climbs from Breckenridge to the ridge.

hike in Breckenridge can be a culinary dream for hikers. Weary travelers have a good selection of restaurants for a post-hike meal. The hike, however, is excellent from either direction.

This segment of the CDT is part of the 300 miles that the CDT shares with the well-marked Colorado Trail. This section of the Colorado Trail is open to mountain bikes. However, due to the terrain, mountain bike usage on the Divide itself is not common and most of the bikes you encounter will be near the Goldhill Trailhead.

To avoid exposure on the Tenmile Range ridge during afternoon thunderstorms, it is best to start early in the morning and hike one way. It is easiest to park at the Goldhill Trailhead in the morning and take the Summit Stage bus to Copper Mountain and hike back to your car.

While there are a few camping options on either side of the Divide, the middle of the hike is above treeline and offers few protected spots so is not suited to overnighting. Be aware that snow can linger until July or August and can be quite steep and dangerous in parts of this hike. Also, during the spring and early summer, avalanche danger on this hike can be high. Use your judgment and be well versed in backcountry safety before attempting this hike when snow lingers, especially before July or after October.

Liz Thomas on the ridgewalk on the Tenmile Range.

PHOTO BY LIZ THOMAS

GETTING THERE: Choose the option that will work best for you:

1. *To get to the Goldhill Trailhead by car:* From the Denver area, take Interstate 70 west. Take Exit 203 (Frisco/Breckenridge). Follow Colorado Highway 9, go through town, and continue south for approximately 6 miles. Turn left on Gateway Drive and the Goldhill Trailhead parking is immediately on the right.

2. *To get to the Copper Mountain Far East Lot Trailhead by car:* From the Denver area, take Interstate 70 west. Take Exit 195 (Copper Mountain/Leadville/Colorado 91) and follow it for 1.1 miles until you see an entrance to the large East End Parking Area. Although it sometimes looks closed off in the summer, there is dedicated parking specifically for CDT and Colorado Trail (CT) hikers toward the far eastern edge of the lot behind an island of trees in the parking lot. You will see CDT signs and a kiosk near the parking area. Do not park where the CDT/CT crosses Colorado 91 about 0.5 mile past the East End Parking area. There is no legal parking along the road there.

3. *To get to the Goldhill Trailhead by Summit Stage bus:* From the Breckenridge Main Transit Center, board the Summit Stage Main Line Route between Frisco and Breckenridge and get off at the Tiger Run stop. Cross Colorado 9 to the west side of the road and walk north (right) along the Blue River Bikeway (which is actually the CDT in this section) for 0.2 mile until you reach Gateway Drive. Turn west (left) and you will see the sign for the CDT/Colorado Trail on your left. If you leave your car at the Goldhill Trailhead, there is a Tiger Run bus stop on the west side of the Colorado 9; this will take you directly into Breckenridge.

4. *To get to the Copper Mountain Trailhead by Summit Stage bus:* From the Breckenridge Main Transit Center, board the Summit Stage main line route between Frisco and Breckenridge. From Frisco Station, board the Copper Mountain Route to the Copper Mountain entrance stop (in summer 2015, it was Stop 8). Cross to the east side of Colorado 91 to the enormous East End parking lot. Walk south along the edge of the parking lot for 0.2 mile until you see the CDT/Colorado Trail (CT) signs and kiosk. Follow the spur trail for 0.1 mile to the paved bike path, which is the CDT.

THE ROUTE: Although this hike starts near the busy Copper Mountain Resort, it quickly becomes peaceful. Walk the 0.1-mile spur trail to a T intersection with the paved bike path, where you will see a CDT sign. Turn left onto the paved bike trail and cross over the beautiful Tenmile Creek on a solid bike trail bridge. Be sure to fill your bottles here as the route solidly climbs for the next few miles. Right after the bridge, you will see a CDT/CT sign indicating you should turn right off the paved bike path and onto a dirt singletrack trail.

Ascend a well-defined trail for 2.0 miles until you reach the Wheeler Intersection. You will gain more than 1,400 feet over generally well-graded terrain. This climb is shaded by a conifer forest and weaves past a few seasonal streams. There are limited camping options available. Take advantage of water and flat spots while you can. You may not find either on the Divide.

At the intersection, make a sharp turn north (left) and continue for 0.5 mile to treeline, climbing steeply. There are ten peaks within the Tenmile Crest and the so-called Peak 8 is just east of you.

From here, prepare yourself for an incredible ridge walk. You will reach treeline just west of Peak 7. Stay along the crest, skirting to the west of Peak 6 (12,573 feet). Snow may linger until July in this area, and the Tenmile Crest is among the first places on the CDT where snow sticks in the autumn. To the north lies Lake Dillon and the town of Dillon. Copper Mountain is 2,500 feet below you to the west. Breckenridge is visible to the east.

At 4.8 miles into the hike, you will reach the high point of the day's journey at 12,495 feet. Continue along the ridge, generally heading north. The trail passes east of Peak 5, then Peak 4, and then Peak 3, before it heads sharply west below Miners Peak (12,923 feet).

You will reach the first crossing of Miners Creek 6.8 miles into the hike. Use this opportunity to fill up your water bottles and revel in the incredible views you just experienced. There are numerous camping opportunities in this area.

As you descend, you will cross water several times. At the Peaks Trail Junction, turn left (north) onto the Peaks Trail for 0.3 mile before turning right (northeast) off of it to stay on the CDT/CT. You will notice that the trees here appear younger. Goldhill was once logged and you will see the impact of old clear-cuts on the landscape. The mountain pine beetle has further impacted the conifer forest here, although the Forest Service has taken action to clear out some of the dying trees and downed wood from the area.

Although there are several intersections—sometimes with jeep trails—on this side of the range, the CDT/CT is generally well marked. Just 1.0 mile from the Goldhill Trailhead, pay attention to a three-way intersection. The CDT should be well marked with Colorado Trail signs. Head right and descend to the Goldhill Trailhead.

To take the Summit Stage bus to Breckenridge, take a right on the bike path for 0.25 mile to the Tiger Run bus shelter. If you have to return to Copper Mountain to retrieve a car, take the Summit Stage bus back to Breckenridge, and from there take the main line route bus to Frisco and transfer to the bus going to Copper Mountain. The buses run frequently and late into the night, so there are abundant transportation options available for hikers, even after enjoying a meal in Breckenridge.

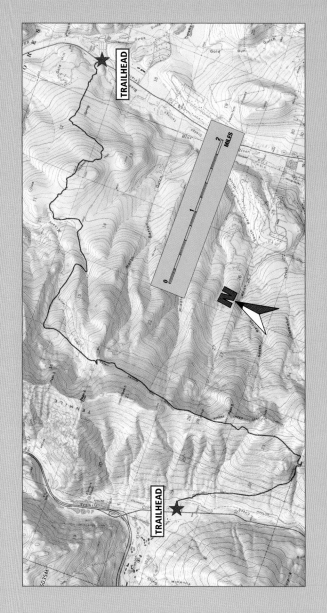

TENMILE RANGE 83

11. Camp Hale to Kokomo Pass

MAPS	Trails Illustrated, Breckenridge/ Tennessee Pass, Number 109; Continental Divide Scenic Trail Map Book: Colorado, Bear Creek Survey, Maps 49–50, Segments 25–26; Guthook App Mile 1208.7 (or 1207.9 if starting at the Lower Camp Hale Trailhead) to 1212.8
ELEVATION GAIN	2,900 feet
RATING	Moderate (or difficult if starting from Lower Camp Hale Trailhead), or as an easy overnighter
ROUND-TRIP DISTANCE	8.4 miles (12.1 miles if starting from Lower Camp Hale Trailhead)
ROUND-TRIP TIME	6 hours (8 hours)
NEAREST LANDMARK	Tennessee Pass

COMMENT: For the history buff, waterfall enthusiast, or high tundra traveler, the hike from Camp Hale to Kokomo Pass offers something for every kind of hiker.

The hike starts at Camp Hale, home and training grounds for the famed 10th Mountain Division, which prepared World War II soldiers for skiing, rock climbing, and winter travel. The division fought in Italy's Apennine Mountains and was responsible for winning two strategic battles in the war. The division sustained casualties as high as 25 percent—some of the highest rates of any unit. Skiing was not then popular in Colorado but many 10th Mountain Division veterans returned to Colorado to help establish the state's fledgling ski industry. Most of the Camp Hale buildings were abandoned and eventually demolished in 1963. From the trailhead, CDT hikers can walk south past the barracks, which are among few remaining buildings. Hikers should take care when camping at this trailhead as

A sign clearly marks the top of Kokomo Pass.   PHOTO BY LIZ THOMAS

there are still undiscovered munitions in the area. Camping is prohibited from Cataract Creek to the South Fork of the Eagle River. An established Forest Service campground is available nearby (directions below).

This hike also offers extraordinary views of the Mount of the Holy Cross (14,011 feet), a peak in the northern Sawatch Range, once one of the most famous mountains in the United States. In the early 1800s, explorers told of a mountain with a giant cross on its side, but were unable to recall its exact location. For more than 50 years, surveyors sought to find the mountain with the cross. In 1873, F.V. Hayden spotted the peak and summitted it. It is likely, however, that undocumented summits by Native Americans predated Hayden. Famous photographer W.H. Jackson (who joined Hayden on the "first" ascent) and famous painter Thomas Moran both created popular images of the mountain. Henry Wadsworth Longfellow wrote a poem, "The Cross of Snow," about it. Thousands traveled to Colorado for pilgrimages to the Mount and the 14er briefly held National Monument status. Fittingly, the first winter ascent of the Mount was made in 1943 by Russell Keene and Howard Freedman, two 10th Mountain Division soldiers.

Despite a short growing season, small tundra flowers flourish on Kokomo Pass. PHOTO BY JOHNNY "BIGFOOT" CARR

Below are two options for starting the hike. For a shorter hike, park at the Upper Camp Hale Trailhead, the old CDT Trailhead before the trail was relocated off Forest Service 714. For a longer hike, park at the Lower Camp Hale Trailhead, which has designated parking spots and is a short walk from the barracks.

GETTING THERE: *To the Lower Camp Hale Trailhead (longer hike):* From Leadville, take US 24 west for 14.4 miles. Turn right onto the 10th Mountain Division Highway and continue for 300 feet. Turn right onto a good dirt road, the Camp Hale Spur 1B, and follow this for 0.5 mile. Turn right onto E. Fork Eagle Road (Forest Service 714) and follow this for 1.5 miles. On your left is a parking lot that holds about five cars.

To the Upper Camp Hale Trailhead: From the lower trailhead, continue on E. Fork Eagle Road (Forest Service 714), heading east for 0.6 mile. You will see the CDT on your left as it joins the road briefly and then heads back into the woods on the left. Continue on FS 714 for another 0.9 mile. On your right, you will see the remnants of a jeep road and on the left, shortly after, you will see a jeep road. Park anywhere along the road. If FS 714 makes a sharp turn right (south), you have gone too far. From the parking area, walk 0.1 mile on a wide trail/jeep road and turn right on the CDT to head towards Kokomo Pass.

To the Camp Hale Memorial Campground: From Leadville, take US 24 west for 14.4 miles. Make a right onto the 10th Mountain Division Highway and continue for 300 feet. Make a right onto Camp Hale Spur 1B and follow this for 0.2 mile. Take the first right onto Forest Service 716. Follow this for 1.2 miles, following the Eagle River and passing the Camp Hale Pond on your left. Turn left onto Forest Road 7161A to the campground.

THE ROUTE: If you parked at the Lower Camp Hale Trailhead (9,362 feet) near Forest Service Road 714, walk north for 0.1 mile along a dirt road to a CDT/Colorado Trail sign on the right side of the road leading to trail heading east. Continue through lightly forested aspen and grassland on mostly flat terrain as you head east on the trail for 0.5 mile.

The trail meets FS Road 714. Make a slight left to walk on the road for 0.15 mile, continuing east until the trail continues on the left, ascending slightly. If you pass a Y in the dirt road, you have gone too far.

Stay on the trail as it traces the flanks of a slope to the north. After 0.7 mile, you will reach beautiful Cataract Falls—one of few waterfalls along the CDT in Colorado—and cross Cataract Creek on a bridge (9,700 feet). Shortly after, you will reach an intersection. If you

July is peak wildflower season near Kokomo Pass.

PHOTO BY JOHNNY "BIGFOOT" CARR

head right along the wide trail for 0.2 mile, you will reach the Upper Camp Hale parking lot. To continue to Kokomo Pass, continue on the trail left/straight near a stream, heading east. (If you started at the Upper Camp Hale parking lot, turn right onto the CDT toward Kokomo Pass).

Climb through one of the most beautiful groves of aspen on the entire CDT. The trail heads east for 0.2 mile before heading north for 0.3 mile. You will come to an intersection with a jeep road. Follow signs for the CDT/CT to continue up a switchback. The trail continues to climb up switchbacks to Cataract Creek—the same creek you crossed on a bridge earlier in the hike. The trail follows the waterway, and you will cross it several times. There are a few places to set up a tent and camp for the night near the creek.

At 5.1 miles into the hike, you will reach treeline and the top of the switchbacks at 11,650 feet. Here, you will walk on tundra, generally heading east for 0.5 mile. You may spot playful but troublesome marmots or the cute and increasingly rare pika, which studies show can die after six hours of exposure to temperatures above 25.5 °C (77.9 °F). The pika is considered by many scientists to be a "canary in the coal mine" for rising temperatures in the American West. From here, be sure to look west and across the valley at the Mount of the Holy Cross in the northern Sawatch Range.

Continue above treeline for 1.4 miles to the signed Kokomo Pass (12,023 feet). North Sheep Mountain (12,415 feet) is to the southeast, with Sheep Mountain (12,329 feet) to the south and East Sheep Mountain (11,870 feet) to the southeast. You will have excellent views across Elk Ridge, which tops out 0.6 mile to the northeast at 12,282 feet. Hikers wanting more high tundra walking, when thunderstorms are not an issue, can continue on the trail all the way to Searle Pass 3.4 miles away, with minor elevation change. Otherwise, enjoy a snack break at Kokomo Pass and retrace your steps back to your car.

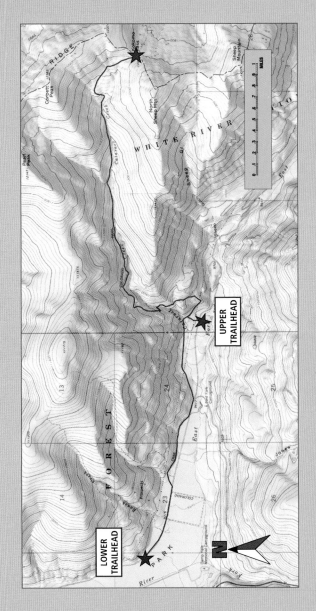

12. Porcupine Lakes (Holy Cross Wilderness)

MAPS	Trails Illustrated, Breckenridge/ Tennessee Pass, Number 109; Continental Divide Scenic Trail Map Book: Colorado, Bear Creek Survey, Map 12, Segments 5–6; Guthook App Mile: 1197.5 to 1192.5
ELEVATION GAIN	1,365 feet
RATING	Easy–moderate, or as an easy overnighter
ROUND-TRIP DISTANCE	10.4 miles
ROUND-TRIP TIME	6 hours, or as an easy overnighter
NEAREST LANDMARK	Wurts Ditch, Colorado Trail Trailhead parking area

COMMENT: This section of the CDT shows off many of Colorado's stunning 14,000-foot peaks, without requiring hikers to do 14er-style climbing. This well-marked, well-defined trail travels through beautiful conifer forests, and with relatively little climbing, you will be rewarded with a tundra walk and excellent views of the Divide. From Tennessee Pass to Twin Lakes, the Divide itself follows the backbones of the massive 14ers in this area, and the CDT travels just below the Divide, providing hikers with classic Colorado views of the Mosquito and Sawatch Ranges. Porcupine Lake is often named by CDT and Colorado Trail (CT) hikers as one of the best alpine camping areas anywhere along the trail.

This area is home to the 10th Mountain Division Hut Association ski huts, which create a network of 29 shelters connected by 300 miles of trails for backcountry hikers, skiers, snowshoers, and snowboarders. The huts are named after the famed 10th Mountain Division soldiers, who trained on these mountains before entering battle in alpine

Porcupine Lakes makes a worthy destination.

Europe during WWII (see the Camp Hale hike comments in Hike 11 to learn more about their history).

Patterned after the European hut-to-hut hiking model, the accommodations found in the huts are rustic, with wood stoves, mattresses and utensils, and a communal kitchen and dining area. The huts are open both winter and summer for hikers, but reservations are required. Although this trip does not pass directly by the huts, you will see signs indicating where the huts are near the CDT. You can learn more about the huts by visiting www.huts.org or calling 970-925-5775.

This section of trail was constructed in the 1930s by the Civilian Conservation Corps and was called the Main Range Trail. Its primary purpose was to provide access for firefighting because scientists at the time believed that forest health was best maintained by fighting all forest fires. Now, forest scientists recognize that wildfire is a natural part of the forest life cycle, and the trail is used primarily for recreation as the CDT and CT.

Part of this section of the CDT travels through the Holy Cross Wilderness. The story of how it got its name is interesting (see the Camp Hale to Kokomo Pass comments in Hike 11 to learn more).

The CDT through this section is shared with the Colorado Trail, whose trail marking restrictions require it to have

Brian "Mr. Gorbachev" Davidson enjoys a snowy September hike.

PHOTO BY LIZ THOMAS

more frequent trail signs than the CDT. However, unlike other sections of the CDT that are shared with the CT, this hike will not have mountain bike traffic because it enters a federally designated wilderness.

If you choose to camp near Porcupine Lake, be aware that it is a high alpine campsite and lightning is a possibility. Note that snow lingers longer on the higher altitude portions of the trail than at the trailhead. Always check weather and snow conditions before heading out on any above-treeline trek.

GETTING THERE: From Leadville, drive north on US Highway 24 for 7.5 miles until you reach Wurts Ditch Road (Forest Service Road 705). Although it may not be signed, the intersection is "marked" by an antique piece of yellow machinery—an old road grader. Turn left onto Wurts Ditch Road and follow it for 1.0 mile as it turns to gravel. At an intersection, turn right onto Wurts Ditch Road and follow it for 0.3 mile, where the Colorado Trail crosses the road. You can park on the side of the road here, although there are limited spots.

THE ROUTE: From Wurts Ditch Road, turn left (heading southeast) to take the CDT towards Porcupine Lakes. Follow the trail through conifers on gently rolling trail for 0.9 mile until you cross a jeep road. In 0.25 mile, you will cross the North Fork of Tennessee Creek and the West Tennessee Creek, all on good bridges. This is potentially a good place to camp, especially in the fall when mosquitoes are gone.

The view of Tennessee Pass from the CDT.   PHOTO BY LIZ THOMAS

A hiker travels through flowers in the Holy Cross Wilderness.

PHOTO BY STEVEN "TWINKLE" SHATTUCK

From here, the trail gently ascends a mild grade, following an old jeep road. At 2.4 miles into your hike, look for a poorly marked intersection. Take a right to stay on the CDT as it journeys toward the Holy Cross Wilderness. In 4.2 miles a sign indicates that you are entering wilderness. Be sure to sign the trail register here.

Soon, the conifers become less dense and the views open up. Follow the CDT as it climbs gently up 600 feet into tundra, from where you can best observe the Divide's once-glaciated headwalls. In July, this area is filled with wildflowers. Here, you are walking past 1.2 billion-year-old granite that forms the eastern portion of the Sawatch Range. To the east, you can see the Mosquito Range.

You will reach Porcupine Lake 5.2 miles and a world away from where you parked your car. This high lake is a great place to take a nap, stop for a lunch break, or set up camp. If you choose to basecamp here, you may enjoy continuing south along the CDT for another mile to experience even more great alpine views. When you are ready, turn around and follow the same route back to your car.

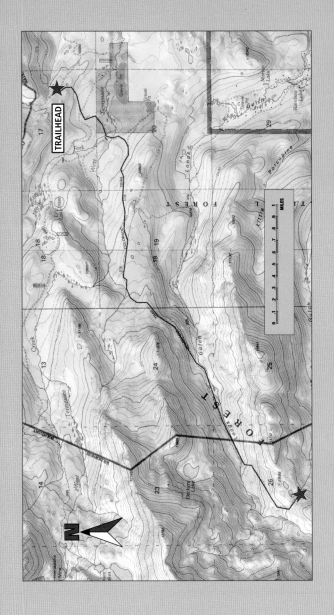

13. Cottonwood Pass to Tincup Pass

MAPS	Trails Illustrated, Buena Vista/ Collegiate Peaks, Number 129; Trails Illustrated, Salida/St. Elmo/ Mount Shavano, 130; Continental Divide Scenic Trail Map Book: Colorado, Bear Creek Survey, Maps 40–42, Segment 21; Guthook App Mile 1124.3 to 1108.4
ELEVATION GAIN	5,867 feet
RATING	Extreme, or as a difficult overnighter
ONE-WAY DISTANCE	15.9 miles
ONE-WAY TRIP TIME	12 hours, or as an overnighter
NEAREST LANDMARK	Cottonwood Pass Road or Tincup Pass Road

COMMENT: This new section of trail, started in 2006 and completed in 2013, highlights some of the true gems of the Collegiate Wilderness and the CDT in Colorado. Although the CDT has always been routed near this area, it previously followed roads. With this new re-route, many long-distance hikers refer to this section as a highlight of the trail in Colorado.

In this section, hikers are rewarded with views of craggy peaks, including 14ers La Plata Peak and Mt. Huron. This route gives hikers top-of-the-world views—indeed, it stays high on the Divide for most of the hike and passes near Mt. Emma Burr, the highest peak on the Divide for 160 miles. Mt. Elbert, the highest peak in Colorado at 14,440 feet, is just a few miles away.

This particular segment was built with funds from part of a large statewide grant from Great Outdoors Colorado

A thru-hiker walks through fields of flowers on his way north to Cottonwood Pass. PHOTO BY JOHNNY "BIGFOOT" CARR

(GOCO) and Colorado State Parks, with additional federal and private funding. The CDT in this section was completed with the help of volunteers, youth groups, and trail enthusiasts like you. The section of this hike from Kreutzer Nose to the ridge on Mount Emma Burr was constructed by Rocky Mountain Youth Corps and the Buena Vista Correctional Facility Trail Crew.

As this section is above treeline, it is best to hike it in the morning and avoid exposure to typical Colorado afternoon thunderstorms. Also, with the route above treeline for so long, you won't likely find water until 11.5 miles into the hike. Many hikers, however, have been able to find snowmelt or smaller intermittent streams along parts of this hike. Although this section is long, there are not many good camping sites along the trail and it is best done as a dayhike. The best time of year for this hike is July to September. Be aware that the roads to the trailheads are not always open, and know that snow can linger on this section well into July. Exercise caution as the trail can be covered with snow and/or be icy. Hikers should check the local conditions and carry appropriate gear.

An epic day of hiking winds down with a glorious sunset reflected in a pond at Cottonwood Pass.

PHOTO BY JOHNNY "BIGFOOT" CARR

GETTING THERE: *To get to Cottonwood Pass:* From Buena Vista, take Chaffee County 306 west for 18.4 miles. The majority of the road is paved except after Taylor Park Reservoir, where it turns to gravel. Note that the road is closed during the winter and usually is open from May until October. A kiosk marks the trailhead, which is at the physical pass. There is parking for six to eight cars.

To get to the Tincup Trailhead: From the town of St. Elmo, follow a dirt road west out of town. After crossing a bridge, turn left and go for 0.25 mile before turning right onto Forest Service Road 267 (Tincup Pass Road or Tincup Access Road). Follow this road for 4.2 miles. The trailhead will be on your left, with room for three to four cars. There is dispersed camping along Tincup Road, with good sites just west of the trail junction.

The Tincup Pass Road is not plowed in the spring and is clear only when the snow melts. Check local conditions to determine whether the road is passable.

If you are setting up a car shuttle between Cottonwood Pass and Tincup Pass Road, note that some GPS or internet mapping systems may suggest taking a route through the National Forest on a mix of dirt, county, and Forest Service roads. This route is much rougher and involves several unmarked road intersections, which can be confusing. Additionally, this route is not plowed and snow can linger into July. Most important, any access to the Tunnel Lake Trailhead/Tincup Pass Road requires a high clearance, four-wheel-drive vehicle.

THE ROUTE: Start at Cottonwood Pass (12,126 feet), following the well-marked trail above treeline. Ascend via switchbacks to a high point a little more than 0.5 mile into the hike. Follow the ridge and the Divide, descending slightly to a saddle—with great views looking towards a small alpine tarn to the south.

After 1.5 miles, climb slightly just below another hill until you reach another saddle. You will cross back and forth over the Divide several times during this hike, each time offering you slightly different views of the basins in the area.

The climbing will become steeper for 0.7 mile as you again ascend the Divide below an unnamed point (12,792 feet). Take a breather to observe Lost Lake, 600 feet below the trail to the east. This alpine tarn is hidden from view from the north and south. Hikers wanting a campsite or in need of water can easily drop down to the lake.

At 2.5 miles into the hike, climb switchbacks to cross over the ridge and cross back again. Now you can enjoy easy and pleasant walking above treeline for the next 0.4 mile as you descend towards a saddle. Climb slightly, contouring a hill, and then contour the flanks well below the peak of an unnamed feature (13,850 feet).

Approximately 4.5 miles into the hike, you will switchback back up towards the Divide. Over the next mile, you will ascend towards a saddle on the ridge south of an unnamed point (13,055 feet). At 5.5 miles into the hike, you return again to the western side of the Divide. Enjoy fantastic views into Mineral Basin and the headwaters of the South Cottonwood Creek. A small unnamed tarn is visible to the north of the basin.

The Divide around you is steep, but the trail takes the gentlest path on the way down. Be aware that snow can linger here late into the season. The trail contours briefly northeast for 0.1 mile before jutting abruptly south and descending for 0.9 mile to more switchbacks. If you reach this section early in the season, it will likely still be covered in snow. Descend the switchbacks and, 0.25 mile later, you will pass a small stream—the first reliable water source.

The trail contours for another 0.75 mile, making a half circle around the eastern flank of Mount Kreutzer (13,095 feet) before heading south, paralleling the divide to the west.

At 9.0 miles into the hike, you will start a slow, gradual climb over the next 0.5 mile to a high point on a saddle just east and below an unnamed point (12,502 feet). Some of the trail through this area crosses through scree fields, but the tread is smooth, thanks to the hand-crushed rock added by trail crews. The walk through this area is exceptional and makes for a sublime hiking experience. Once at the pass, to the east, you will see Mineral Creek and a jeep road. To the west is Emma Burr Mountain, at 13,544 feet the tallest peak on the Divide in 160 miles. Although it is unclear who Emma Burr was, she is one of a dozen or so women immortalized in mountain names in Colorado.

Descend switchbacks for 0.25 mile and continue to follow the trail heading south. Approximately 10.8 miles into the hike, you will cross the headwaters of Morgan Gulch before ascending for 0.3 mile via switchbacks to a ridge. The trail then descends gradually, continuing south, then southeast. At 12.2 miles into the hike, make an abrupt turn west for 0.25 mile before descending a series of switchbacks aimed south towards treeline. At 13 miles into the hike, you reach treeline, still descending on switchbacks for 1.0 mile. At 14 miles, the trail gradually descends through forest towards Chalk Creek. At 15.9 miles, you have reached the intersection with the Tincup Pass jeep road and the end of this spectacular section.

Boreal toad

The Boreal toad (*Anaxyrus boreas boreas*) lives between 7,000 and 12,000 feet and is a listed as an endangered species by the States of Colorado and New Mexico. It lives in the southern Rocky Mountains. It has experienced dramatic population declines over the past two decades related to disease and habitat loss. It is a very rare treat to see the toad. If you spot a toad, please refrain from touching it or altering its habitat.

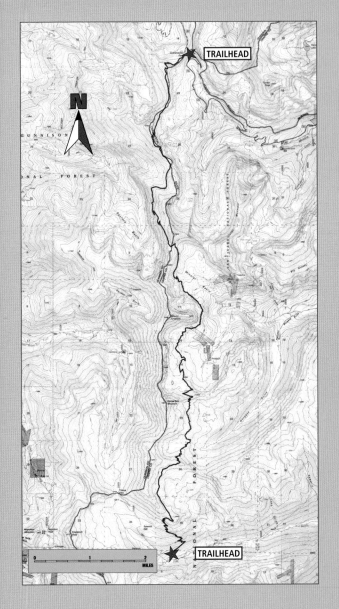

TRAILHEAD

N

TRAILHEAD

0   1   2
MILES

14. Monarch Pass Loop

BY KARL LUCE & CDTC CONTRIBUTORS

MAPS	Trails Illustrated, Salida/St. Elmo/ Mount Shavano, Number 130; Trails Illustrated, La Garita/ Cochetopa Hills, Number 139; Continental Divide Scenic Trail Map Book: Colorado, Bear Creek Survey, Map 36, Segment 18; Guthook App Mile 1082.4 to 1084
ELEVATION GAIN	856 feet
RATING	Family friendly
ROUND-TRIP DISTANCE	2.5 miles
ROUND-TRIP TIME	2 hours
NEAREST LANDMARK	Monarch Crest Store

COMMENT: Monarch Pass has played an important role in Colorado's development for travel over the Continental Divide. Going back to the 1880s, there have been two other "official" Monarch Passes located to the west and northwest of the current Monarch Pass (both on the Divide). They are frequently referred to as Old Monarch Pass and Old, Old Monarch Pass. Old, Old Monarch Pass, at the westernmost reaches of adjacent Monarch Ski Area, served as the crossing for a stage road. It guided the flow of miners from the old Monarch mining camp to Gunnison Basin camps.

In 1878, what was once a collection of ramshackle tents and cabins on the east side of Monarch Pass was grubstaked by Nicholas C. Creede. Eventually, the site was platted into a city, with over one hundred houses, three hotels, and the usual assortment of saloons and brothels. It was named Chaffee City in 1880, in honor of Jerome B. Chaffee, who had worked hard for statehood and who was Colorado's

On this family-friendly hike, you get excellent views of the range the CDT continues into.

PHOTO BY JOHNNY "BIGFOOT" CARR

first senator. The name was changed to Monarch in 1894. Monarch came to an abrupt end in the panic of '93 and never recovered.

Old Monarch Pass became the next "official" crossing—as part of a transcontinental automobile route in the 1920s. The present "official" Monarch Pass was opened in 1939 as the brainchild of Charles Vail. Mr. Vail had the audacity to name the pass after himself. The locals protested and even vandalized the Vail sign until the name was changed to reflect local history.

There are also rich associations here with the Ute Indians, via the names of local peaks. The great Chief Ouray; his wife Chipeta; and Shavano, leader of the Tabeguache band, are honored in this fashion. US Route 50 now winds through the pass. This is also the site of the Monarch Crest tourist shop and an aerial tram (both open during the summer season).

The hike described here starts from the Monarch Crest parking lot to the south, along US Route 50, before cutting diagonally upslope to the south-southwest. Its approach is part of a CDT relocation created in 2008 and guides the

Old Monarch Pass is right on the Continental Divide.

PHOTO BY PHIL "NOWHERE MAN" HOUGH

hiker gently up to the western slopes of the Continental Divide, before taking a turn to the northwest. The trail continues its somewhat level grade until reaching the Old Monarch Pass Road (Forest Road 237). It then departs from the current CDT to attain Old Monarch Pass and a meeting with an older single-track trail, also known as the Crest Trail (#531). Finish the loop by following the Crest Trail (also the route of the older CDT section) back to Monarch Pass and the parking lot.

The route is well graded for the most part and is a great option for families. It winds in and out of conifers and onto open slopes with views to the west into the Gunnison Basin and north towards the Monarch Ski Area. Restroom facilities and water are available at the pass, as well as the tourist-friendly souvenir shop, snack bar, and educational displays. Folks not wanting to hike but still wanting to enjoy panoramic views can purchase a journey up the quaint gondola 750 feet to the east of the pass.

In July, wildflowers dot the side of the trail. PHOTO BY JOHNNY "BIGFOOT" CARR

GETTING THERE: From Poncha Springs, take US Route 50 west from its northernmost intersection with US Route 285 for 18 miles to the top of Monarch Pass (11,386 feet). From Gunnison, take US Route 50 east for 45 miles to Monarch Pass. Ample parking near the Monarch Crest store is available on the east side of US 50.

THE ROUTE: From the Monarch Crest parking lot, carefully cross US 50 to its west side and walk south for 0.1 mile. The CDT departs right from US 50 up an embankment. Immediately approach a trailhead kiosk and head to the left on the official and current CDT. (The trail branching to your right is the older CDT and part of Crest Trail #531.) The well-graded trail gradually ascends and, after 0.2 mile, reaches the western slope of the Continental Divide.

Deb "Walking Carrot" Hunsicker at Monarch Pass ready to hike.

Continuing around the shoulder, the CDT aligns itself northwest at a relatively constant elevation through conifers. Keep an eye out for squirrels and chipmunks who will scold you for interrupting their work collecting seeds. You may also admire the views to the left down into Porphyry Park and Porphyry Creek.

After 0.8 mile of contouring, the trail intersects the maintained dirt Old Monarch Pass Road (Forest Road 237). Turn right and descend 0.5 mile along FR 237 to an intersection with the old CDT route and Crest Trail (#531).

Turn right onto the Crest Trail and climb up a steep intermediate hill for 0.2 mile, followed by a drop to a notch. You will now encounter a final climb on open slopes while aiming for the left of the next, and last, summit, while staying above timberline. The final descent along the ridge overlooks the lodge at Monarch Pass and returns to the trailhead kiosk where the old and new CDT split. Follow US 50 north back to the Monarch Crest parking lot.

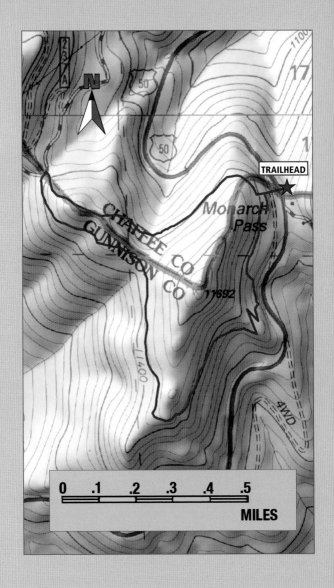

TRAILHEAD

Monarch
Pass

CHAFFEE CO
GUNNISON CO

11692

11400

4WD

0	.1	.2	.3	.4	.5

MILES

15. Snow Mesa

MAPS	Trails Illustrated, La Garita/ Cochetopa Hills, Number 139 Continental Divide Scenic Trail Map Book: Colorado, Bear Creek Survey, Map 22, Segment 12; Guthook App 981.9 to 987.0
ELEVATION GAIN	1,744 feet (one-way to end of the mesa)
RATING	Easy (with moderate option to the end of the mesa)
ROUND-TRIP DISTANCE	4 miles (with 10.6-mile option)
ROUND-TRIP TIME	3 to 6 hours
NEAREST LANDMARK	Willow Creek Pass Parking Area

COMMENT: If you've ever wanted to feel the remoteness of "walking on the moon," the hike up to Snow Mesa is a great option. The 4.5-mile-wide Snow Mesa, above Spring Creek, provides unobscured views of isolated CDT country in southern Colorado—including the San Juans, the Rio Grande Pyramid, and the Uncompahgre Mountains.

Although Snow Mesa is relatively close to a road, it feels isolated. Do not be surprised to spot elk, or even sheep dogs, shepherds, and large flocks of sheep. Walking this section gives you a taste of the Colorado high country much as it must have been in the days of the Old West.

Although the map makes Snow Mesa appear flat, the trail dips in and out of creek drainages, which provide hikers with water sources. However, as the mesa is quite exposed, there are not many sheltered camping spots. Nevertheless, on a clear night with low winds, camping on the mesa can provide you with unbeatable star viewing.

The magic of this hike is that, once you are on the mesa, you can just ramble along the top—there is no need to walk all the way to the end. As with any hike in this book, choose

The mesa may look flat, but it is actually 1,200 feet above the pass.

PHOTO BY STEVEN "TWINKLE" SHATTUCK

your own turnaround point based on weather conditions, your fitness level, and your interest in continuing on. Thus, this hike can be as short as 4 miles, if you climb to the top of the mesa for the views, or as long as 10 miles, if you walk to the end of the mesa and back.

Note that this section of the CDT is shared with the well-marked Colorado Trail and is open to mountain bikes. Due to the rocky terrain, all but the strongest riders will be walking their bikes on the uphill, but be alert for cyclists coming downhill. The visibility on the mesa should allow for plenty of warning if a bike is approaching.

Once atop the mesa, there is no shelter available and it can be an exposed and scary place on windy days, especially during lightning storms. Plan your trip to be safely off the mesa during the afternoon, when thunderstorms are most likely to occur. Always check the weather before heading out on this trip.

GETTING THERE: *To reach the Spring Creek Pass Trailhead:* From Lake City, take Colorado 149 southeast for 17 miles to the Spring Creek Pass Trailhead. From Creede, take

Colorado 149 northwest for 33 miles to reach Spring Creek Pass Trailhead.

At the pass, there is parking for about a dozen cars, plus picnic tables, a pit toilet, fire rings, and an information kiosk. Hikers wanting an early start can easily camp nearby. Although water is available from a ditch near the road in a pinch, such water may be contaminated. If possible, bring enough water for your party to camp and reach the first water source on the mesa. Regardless of the source, it is always wise to purify water before drinking it.

THE ROUTE: Start right on the Continental Divide at Spring Creek Pass. Cross to the east side of the highway and follow signs to the CDT Trailhead (10,908 feet). The trail climbs, sometimes steeply, for 1.6 miles through conifers as you gain more than 1,200 feet. The trail here can be quite rocky. You will reach treeline at 11,880 feet.

Climb a short bowl for 0.4 mile to the top of the mesa. You should be able to see a post at the edge of the mesa (12,260 feet). From here, the views should be incredible and it is easy to forget that you are only 2 miles from your car. You will have the rewarding experience of seeing the trail for miles.

If you are satisfied with your hike here, you can turn around and head back to your car. Otherwise, continue along the CDT, following posts and walking on good trail tread headed generally east.

Over the course of the next 2.0 miles, the trail remains generally at the same elevation, but you will drop in and out of six different creek drainages. At times, the climb in and out of these creeks can be steep, but they also provide you with water sources to refill bottles and take relaxing breaks.

The mesa ends near a pond that is 5.3 miles from your car. From here, the CDT makes a sharp left turn and heads north toward the La Garita Wilderness. After enjoying the beauty of this rare pond on Snow Mesa, turn around and retrace your steps back to Spring Creek Pass.

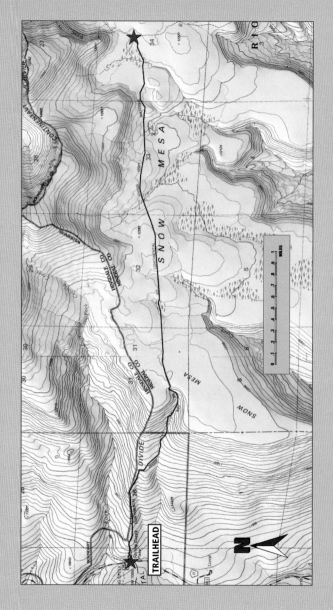

TRAILHEAD

N

MILES

16. Cataract Ridge

MAPS	Trails Illustrated, Telluride/Silverton/Ouray/Lake City, Number 141; Continental Divide Scenic Trail Map Book: Colorado, Bear Creek Survey, Map 19, Segment 10; Guthook App Mile 964.7 to 940.7
ELEVATION GAIN	3,515 feet
RATING	Difficult, or as an easy–moderate overnighter
ONE-WAY DISTANCE	15.9 miles
ONE-WAY TRIP TIME	10 hours to multi-day
NEAREST LANDMARK	Stony Pass

COMMENT: One of the most iconic parts of the whole CDT and the Colorado Trail, Cataract Ridge is known for its remoteness, wildlife viewing opportunities, and CDT views. This is one of those places where you can't take a bad photograph. It is not uncommon to see moose, bighorn sheep, elk, marmots, and pika on Cataract Ridge. The hike takes you past the headwaters of one of the most important waterways in America, the Rio Grande.

Sections of this trail require you to follow cairns, and those who find beauty in giant cairn construction will find in this section some of the most beautiful pieces of rock art on the whole CDT.

History buffs will enjoy finishing the hike at Stony Pass Road, which was built in 1879 to transport ore and supplies between the mines and the town of Silverton. The road was popular until 1882, when the Denver and Rio Grande Western's rail line through the Animas Canyon—which still runs as a tourist line—became a much easier route between Silverton and the mines. The road fell into disrepair, but is still very popular with four-wheelers, who describe Stony

It doesn't get much better than life above treeline on a beautiful day in the San Juans. PHOTO BY JOHNNY "BIGFOOT" CARR

Pass Road as one of the longest uninterrupted climbs in Colorado. The ghost town of Beartown is near Stony Pass and some interpretative signs share the history of the area.

Although almost all of this hike is above 12,000 feet, and it is extremely remote, Cataract Ridge has plenty of water, is relatively short, and has less elevation gain than other comparable sections of the CDT in Colorado. As a result, although by no means "easy," this hike (along with the longer-mileage Cumbres Pass to Blue Lake hike) could be a good option for introducing friends and family to backpacking.

GETTING THERE: Note that both trailheads are only accessible by high clearance four-wheel-drive vehicles.

To get to Carson Saddle: From Lake City, take Colorado 149 south for 1.5 miles to a Y in the road. Take a right onto County Road 30, following signs to Lake San Cristobal. Continue on this road for 9.3 miles, passing the lake about halfway through. About a mile past another set of lakes, the Castle Lakes, you will see a dirt road to the left, which is Wager Gulch Road. If you cross a bridge over Lake Fork, you have gone too far. Turn left on Wager Gulch Road (BLM Road 3308/Forest Service Road 562/County Road 36), staying left when the road splits about 400 feet after turning off County Road 30 (the road to the right dead-ends). This road is very steep and rocky and has many hairpin turns, mak-

The CDT through this section is well marked and signed.

ing it popular with ATVs and motorcycles. Continue for 5.0 miles until you reach Carson Saddle.

To get to Stony Pass/Beartown Trailhead: From Silverton, take the right branch of Colorado 110, following signs to Howardsville (ignore Colorado Highway 110 left, which leads to the Silverton Ski Area). It will turn into County Road 2. Follow this for 4.1 miles to Howardsville and then turn right onto Stony Pass Road (County Road 4/FS Road 589). Follow FS Road 589 for 2 miles and turn left on FS Road 737/County Road 3 to climb up from the Animas Valley via switchbacks. After about a mile, turn right at

a T intersection to stay on County Road 3 (the left turn dead-ends). Follow the road for 2.0 miles and you will be at Stony Pass. There is a small parking lot and interpretative signs on your left.

Note that Carson Pass and Stony Pass are both popular with off-roaders and many hikers have had luck asking motorists for rides from these points back to Silverton or Lake City.

Climbing towards the pass during a storm.

Small ponds can be useful water sources along the ridgewalk.

THE ROUTE: From Carson Saddle, follow a jeep trail south for 0.5 mile until you reach the singletrack CDT/CT to your right. Climb steeply, and then follow the trail as it bends west (right) and up the Lost Creek Trail watershed. At 0.7 mile later, you will find a small stream with a campsite 50 feet below the trail to the north (left). You will cross two more streams—each about a mile apart—before you top out at unnamed pass 3.7 miles into your hike.

As you climb through the gentle Lost Creek Trail watershed to that unnamed pass, keep an eye out for moose feasting in the willow, as they are frequent visitors to the area. To the north (right) is Bent Peak (13,393 feet) and further northwest is Carson Peak (13,657 feet). Most likely you won't be able to see the tops, but the trail traverses along both mountains' southern flanks. To your south across the valley are unnamed peaks 12,448', 13,581', and 13,580'.

Celebrating a successful climb to the ridge.   PHOTO BY LIZ THOMAS

At 3.7 miles, you will reach an unnamed pass (12,919 feet) where it is common to spot bighorn sheep. The trail through the Lost Trail Creek watershed is the old La Garita Stock Driveway, and even at this high elevation, cattle can be seen grazing on the tundra vegetation.

From the pass, descend into the Pole Creek drainage, which continues west. At mile 5.0, pay attention to a well-marked intersection where the CDT/Colorado Trail turns right (north) away from a faint trail that once led to the West Lost Trail Creek Trail, which was partially destroyed in a 1991 landslide. Here, the CDT/CT turns away from the Pole Creek Trail, which is the old CDT. The Pole Creek Trail is still used as a bad weather alternate by CDT thru-hikers who wish to avoid high ridges during thunderstorms.

If your weather is good, head west onto the CDT and descend steeply to a small lake, where there are a few campsites available. If you are looking for more campsites, turn right at a trail intersection at the lake and follow a side trail along the northwestern edge of the lake about 0.25 mile north and you will see the much larger Cataract Lake to your right (east).

Otherwise, continue left to stay on the CDT, which follows the southwestern edge of the pond before continuing west.

There are a few more flat spots for camping before you cross a stream and head slightly right, climbing through an open field where you can often see elk. Ascend through a small saddle (12,675 feet) just south of Half Peak (13,481 feet), located 6.8 miles into your hike. The trail heads slightly right (north) and continues to climb, contouring the southwestern flank of the peak. This section is all on good, relatively new trail. Additionally, it is marked with cairns and should be easy to follow, even in light snow.

At 7.8 miles into the hike, pay attention to cairns marking that your trail is turning left (southwest). You will walk for 0.4 mile near a rocky ridge that is home to marmots and pika. The cairns are giant and solidly constructed and you should have no trouble finding them.

Continue to follow cairns down into a valley, reaching the low point 8.5 miles into the hike. Continue straight (west) across the valley and continue back up, ignoring a faint trail that intersects the CDT at the valley floor. At 0.5 mile later, you will drop down, cross a gully, and climb another rolling hill. Continue to follow cairns for 0.8 mile and climb to a pass on the Continental Divide (12,722 feet). From here, the trail rolls up and down along the Divide until the descent at the end of the hike.

Go straight through an intersection 9.9 miles into your hike. Trail tread is visible here, but you can also follow the cairns for another 0.5 mile to another saddle, where you will head straight again. Make a left at an intersection at the pass following signs for the CDT/CT.

At 11.4 miles into the hike, at another pass, continue straight through an intersection with the Minnie Gulch Trail. At 0.25 mile later, climb to a high point just below 13,000 feet and follow cairns as the trail drops to a pass 1.0 mile later, where you will go straight through an intersection with the Maggie Gulch Trail, which heads downhill to your right (north), leading to a road and pit toilet about

Interesting rock formations mark the ascent from Carson Pass.

5.0 miles away. To your left is the West Fork Trail #918, which was formerly the CDT and connects to the Pole Creek Trail you encountered 8.0 miles earlier.

Stay straight to continue on the new CDT as it passes a small pond 13.5 miles into your hike. This is a good place to get some water before climbing to another high point 0.25 mile later. Directly to your west is Canby Mountain (13,478 feet), which will loom over you for the rest of this hike. When the weather is good, summiting Canby Mountain is a popular side trip for many CDT hikers.

Drop to the last saddle of this trip and pay attention for a very important intersection—it should be well signed. Turn left, heading south into a beautiful treeless valley. You will reach a creek 0.3 mile later—but more exciting than just being a water source, this is the headwaters of the mighty Rio Grande River, for which the Rio Grande National Forest, where you are currently standing, is named. You will reach an intersection 0.4 mile later. Turn right to stay on the CDT, contouring a 180-degree clockwise turn around Canby Mountain, staying relatively high on the hillside. You will reach Stony Pass Road 15.5 miles into your hike. Make a right and continue up the road for 0.4 mile to the trailhead where you might have parked your car.

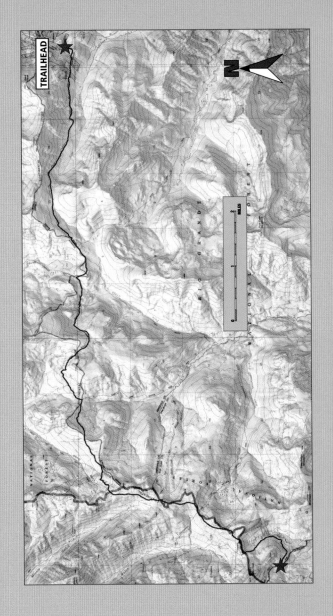

TRAILHEAD

N

2 1 0
MILES

RIO GRANDE NATIONAL FOREST

NATIONAL FOREST

17. Weminuche Window and the Grand Pyramid

MAPS	Trails Illustrated, Weminuche Wilderness, Number 140; Continental Divide Scenic Trail Map Book: Colorado, Bear Creek Survey, Map 15, Segment 7; Guthook App Mile 920.4 to 925.2 (pass near the Window) or 924.2 (lake along the CDT where you can climb to the Window)
ELEVATION GAIN	1,200 feet to Weminuche Pass, 4,045 feet to the Window
RATING	Moderate dayhike to Weminuche Pass, moderate overnighter to the Window
ROUND-TRIP DISTANCE	10.2 miles round-trip to the pass, 22.2 miles round-trip to the Window
ROUND-TRIP TIME	6 hours to the pass, 12 hours to overnighter for the Window
NEAREST LANDMARK	Thirty Mile Campground

COMMENT: This easily accessible, well-maintained section of the wild Weminuche Wilderness shows off two highlight features of the CDT in Colorado: the Window and the Rio Grande Pyramid. This hike accesses the CDT via Weminuche Pass (10,568 feet), the lowest and one of the gentlest passes over the Divide in the Weminuche Wilderness.

The Window, also known as the Devil's Gateway, is a volcanic dike coming off the edge of the Rio Grande Pyramid. An unlikely, square-shaped geologic feature, it is one of the most iconic spots on the CDT. From a distance, the Window looks like a huge gap in the Divide. Hikers can stand inside the Window and observe 100-foot walls standing like towers on either side of the ridge, and view two basins in the other two directions.

From this small lake, climb off-trail through the willows to the Window.

PHOTO BY NANCY HUBER

The Rio Grande Pyramid is one of the few Colorado 13,000-foot peaks that does not have a nearby 14er. As a result, this massive mountain exercises a dominating presence on the landscape. Despite this mountain's beauty, its remote location and the long hike in keep the crowds away.

The hike to Weminuche Pass is moderate, with one short, steep section and many gradual ones. If you choose to go all the way to the Window, you may want to do the hike as an overnighter. Those headed all the way to the Window will have to do some easy off-trail travel. Otherwise, you can get a great view of the Window from the CDT.

The view of the Window from Weminuche Pass.

PHOTO BY JOHNNY "BIGFOOT" CARR

The CDT follows the Rincon La Vaca to a ridge just below Window Peak (13,156 feet) on the Divide. In Spanish, *rincon* means an isolated canyon or corner, and *la vaca* means cow, but you are more likely to see elk or deer in this area.

Although this is one of the lowest points on the CDT in the Weminuche Wilderness, you should still watch for thunderstorms. Please use the free, self sign-in permit at the trailhead to help land managers determine use numbers and to help ensure your party's safety.

GETTING THERE: From Creede, drive 24 miles west on Colorado Highway 149. Turn west (left) onto County Road 18/Forest Road 520 and follow it for 11 miles to the Thirty Mile Campground. There is a parking area for hikers and backpackers in the northwest part of the campground. The trailhead itself is in the south-southwest part of the campground.

THE ROUTE: From the south-southwest part of the Thirty Mile Campground (9,300 feet), start at the Weminuche Creek Trailhead. Not far from the parking lot, the Squaw Creek Trail (#814) branches off to the right. Stay straight on the Weminuche Creek Trail (#818), which stays level, heading south-southwest along the Rio Grande Reservoir dam. The trail contours above the reservoir, through an aspen forest that is beautiful in the fall. Columbines and other wildflowers adorn this area in the spring, and just the walk along the reservoir is a good hike for families.

After about 1.2 miles, make a sharp left to head south up the Weminuche Creek Canyon. The trail will be moderately steep in this area, as it ascends 800 feet over 0.8 mile on rocky terrain. At 1.5 miles into the hike, you will cross the swift-moving Weminuche Creek on a sturdy bridge. Continue climbing up the canyon until you reach broad meadows about 2.0 miles into your hike.

From here, the next 2.0 miles of trail become much gentler as you contour high above Weminuche Creek. You will still be able to get water from several creeks. Crossing these creeks may get your feet wet in the late spring. To your left (west) is Simpson Mountain (12,900 feet).

At 4.5 miles into the hike, you will return to Weminuche Creek. In the early spring, it can be a deep ford, but is usually not dangerous. Shortly after, you will reach Weminuche Pass (10,622 feet), which is a broad, wide meadow pass located 5.1 miles and 1,200 feet from the trailhead.

Near the pass, you will cross a small creek and see two posts marking an intersection with a trail to your right—the unmaintained Skyline or Opal Lake Trail (Trail #564), which was the old CDT. If you are doing this trip as an overnighter, the trees nearby offer a good place to camp.

The Window is a prominent point on the Divide.

PHOTO BY JOHNNY "BIGFOOT" CARR

The ridge near the Window at sunset.   PHOTO BY JOHNNY "BIGFOOT" CARR

Otherwise, stay straight (south) to reach the new and better-maintained CDT.

The trail continues southwest, through a mostly flat meadow paralleling the Raber Lohr Ditch for 0.5 mile, where you will intersect with the new CDT. This area can sometimes be grassy and marshy and the trail can sometimes be obscured. If you lose the trail, keep heading straight (south) until you see the mouth of a drainage on your right.

Follow the CDT as it heads up the Rincon La Vaca. As you hit treeline, you will get your first views of the Rio Grande Pyramid and the Window. Above you to the south are several mesa-like features, Point 12,497 and Point 12,724.

You can access the Window by making a short off-trail detour. When you are above treeline, pass an obvious intersection with the unmaintained Skyline Trail (the same trail you passed at Weminuche Pass). Continue past four creeks (which may not always be flowing). When you reach a small lake/pond with a clear view of the Window right above it, leave the trail. You may need to skirt willows on the left. Head towards the Window, on small rocks and low-lying vegetation, for 0.3 mile, with the Window and your final destination always in view. You may find a use trail heading northwest right between the pillars of the Window. Retrace your steps to return to your vehicle.

> **User-created trails**
> A "use" trail, also referred to as a "social" or "access" trail, is an unofficial trail created by repeated foot use of an area in order to access a notable off-trail area. Such trails can sometimes be useful or necessary, but when possible, we should all avoid creating new ones.

18. Knife Edge

MAPS	Trails Illustrated, Weminuche Wilderness, Number 140; Continental Divide Scenic Trail Map Book: Colorado, Bear Creek Survey, Map 12, Segment 5; Guthook App Mile: 901.0 to 987.3
ELEVATION GAIN	5,377 feet
RATING	Difficult overnighter
ROUND-TRIP DISTANCE	21.1 mile loop
ROUND-TRIP TIME	Overnighter to multi-day
NEAREST LANDMARK	Williams Creek trailhead parking area

COMMENT: The Knife Edge is considered by many people to be the most difficult and terrifying part of the entire CDT. Brave adventurers and thrill seekers can access this memorable CDT section—situated in one of the wildest places in Colorado—as an overnight or fastpacking trip.

The Knife Edge is a quarter-mile-long shelf within a shale rock cliff, right on the Continental Divide. With West Trout Creek half a mile directly below you, and directly above you a cliff hovering over the trail, walking the Knife Edge can be a dizzying and petrifying experience. Throw some snow or ice onto the route, and a wrong move on the Knife Edge can be deadly. Located in the Weminuche Wilderness, the largest wilderness in Colorado, the hike is remote and the stakes are high for the wild risk-takers who dare to travel here.

This loop hike also offers adventurers access to some of the highest country on the CDT, as it travels for many miles above 12,000 feet. In good weather, CDT hikers can see the San Juan mountain range, which has thirteen 14,000-foot peaks. You will pass Williams Lake and come

When covered in snow, the steep traverse across the Knife Edge can be quite treacherous.   PHOTO BY JOHNNY "BIGFOOT" CARR

near Trout Lakes, both of which are well known for good fly fishing.

This section of the CDT is remote and you must hike almost 10 miles on other trails in order to reach the Divide. We chose access trails that are beautiful themselves, and trails that approach the Divide from the south side, because snow melts out more quickly on these trails and hikers have easier access in early summer. This "lollipop" loop is described below in the more gradually ascending clockwise direction. However, it can be hiked counterclockwise as well, which may be preferable for those opting to camp in Palisade Meadows.

The Knife Edge loop is very exposed and afternoon thunderstorms are likely. Always check the weather before starting your trip, evaluate conditions during your hike, and opt to get off of high ridges should you hear thunder closer than 5 miles. Do not be afraid to leave the trail to get off a high ridge—storms move very quickly and the decision could save your life. It is best to get an early morning start. To make this easier, you can take advantage of numerous campgrounds near the trailhead.

Due to the high altitude, snow and ice can linger into July in this section. Be sure to carry the proper gear to safely navigate this kind of terrain and know how to use the gear before heading out. Consider taking a class on winter skills if you plan to be in this section before the snow has melted out. Be prepared to navigate this section in the snow, as the trail may often be obscured by snow.

This hike should only be attempted by those who have the skills, gear, and common sense to make safe decisions while hiking it. The hike itself is long and strenuous with extreme elevation gain, and the altitude of the hike only makes it more difficult. Due to the safety issues on this hike, be sure to leave your itinerary with folks at home and travel in a group. Although the potential for danger on this hike is high, those who safely attempt it will be rewarded with an incredible experience.

GETTING THERE: *To get to campgrounds and the trailhead:* From Pagosa Springs, take US 160 west/San Juan St. for 2.0 miles to Piedra Road. Turn right onto Piedra Road and head north for 15.7 miles. The road will turn into Forest Service Road 631. Continue for 6.2 miles. Turn right onto Forest Road 640. If you are headed to the Williams Creek Campground, continue for 0.3 mile, and make your first right into the Williams Creek Campground loop.

For those heading straight to the trailhead, do not turn right into the campground, but instead continue straight on Forest Service Road 640 for 1.0 mile. At the Y in the road, stay left/straight to continue on FS 640, ignoring

the access road to the Teal Campground and Williams Creek Reservoir. At 0.2 mile later, continue straight on FS 640, ignoring FS 723, another access road to the

The ridgewalk on this hike offers some of the best views in the Weminuche Wilderness.

PHOTO BY JOHNNY "BIGFOOT" CARR

Reservoir. In another 0.8 mile, stay straight/left at the Y to remain on FS 640. In 2.0 miles, reach an intersection with FS 644 and stay straight/right to remain on FS 640. Half a mile later, you will pass Cimaronna Campground on your right before dead-ending a mile later at the Williams Creek Trailhead near the Palisades Horse Campground.

THE ROUTE: Start on the Williams Creek Trail #587 at the trailhead on the northern end of Palisades Horse Campground. After 0.25 mile of gentle grade, you will reach the Weminuche Wilderness. Climb more steeply up switchbacks, traversing well above Williams Creek. You will cross several streams, which may be swift during high snowmelt. After 2.0 miles, you will reach an intersection with the Indian Creek Trail #588 on your right. Stay on the Williams Creek Trail (left), continuing through a meadow, crossing several streams, and then crossing another meadow before returning to the trees and descending to Williams Creek. The trail follows the creek more closely now and you will ford it 3.0 miles into your trip. Ignore a spur trail 0.5 mile later and ford Williams Creek again 0.2 mile later. Travel through an aspen forest, ignoring another spur trail 5.3 miles into the hike. Follow switchbacks up as the trail heads above treeline and contours a rock feature. You will cross another meadow and a few more streams before fording Williams Creek twice more at 6.5 miles and 7.0 miles into the hike.

At 7.6 miles into your hike, you will reach an intersection with the Williams Lake Fork Trail #664 on your right. Turn right (northeast) onto the Williams Lake Fork Trail #664 and climb to the Williams Lakes (11,665 feet), the largest of which is 2.0 miles from the junction with the Williams Creek Trail. The route from here is 2.7 miles up to the CDT, which you will reach at 12,010 feet.

Hikers will find a potential campsite at Williams Lake. Although there are no trees, the bowl offers some protection from the wind. In addition, the fishing here is excellent.

When you reach the Divide, you will have climbed about 3,400 feet from the trailhead. Turn east (right) and you will be on the CDT Trail #813.

From the intersection of the CDT and the Williams Lake Fork Trail, take a moment to admire the scenery before heading onto the Knife Edge. Baldy Mountain (12,477 feet) is to the northeast and Trout Lake is visible to the north. Chief Mountain (12,946 feet) is visible directly to the west. Continue east, ignoring two intersections with trails on your left that head down to Trout Lake and Trout Creek. During peak wildflower season, this section is incredible.

Here, you can see the open promontory of the Knife Edge ahead of you to the east. Evaluate conditions before committing to continue. The Knife Edge is 0.9 mile from the intersection with the Williams Lake Trail. Once past the Knife Edge, continue on the CDT on open tundra as it heads south for 1.1 miles just south of Cherokee Lake. A side trail descends a short distance to the lake.

Ascend a side slope with a lot of vegetation. Here you will find a stream, one of few water sources this high up on the divide.

Continue traversing the Divide on the CDT for 2.3 miles until you reach an intersection with the Palisade Meadows Trail #651 heading south. Make a right onto Trail #651, and descend from the Divide via switchbacks for 2.5 miles to Palisade Meadows. Here, you will hit the Indian Creek Trail #588 at an unsigned intersection. Turn right and head southwest, following Indian Creek as you descend steeply for 0.3 mile to a ford of Indian Creek. Reach another ford 0.4 mile later. Continue southwest on the Indian Creek Trail for 2.0 more miles until you ford Williams Creek. A 90-foot climb and 0.3 mile later, you will hit the Williams Creek Trail—the same trail you started on miles ago. This time, turn left and head southwest for 2.0 miles to return to your car at the Williams Creek Trailhead near the Palisades Horse Campground.

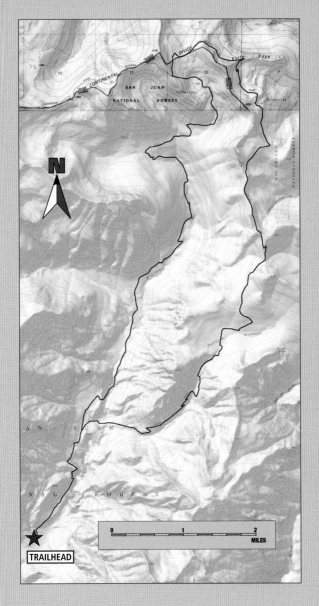

19. Wolf Creek Pass to Rock Lake

MAPS	Trails Illustrated, Weminuche Wilderness, Number 140; Continental Divide Scenic Trail Map Book: Colorado, Bear Creek Survey, Maps 8–9, Segment 4; Guthook App Mile 865.4 to 873.9
ELEVATION GAIN	820 feet
RATING	Easy, or as a family friendly overnighter
ROUND-TRIP DISTANCE	8.8 miles
ROUND-TRIP TIME	5 hours to multi-day
NEAREST LANDMARK	Lobo Overlook

COMMENT: Coloradans have always taken pride in Wolf Creek Pass (10,859 feet), which is the low point in the mountains between some of the wildest and most beautiful country in the state. The name often appears in weather reports, as the pass receives as much as 400 inches of snow annually and is used as an example of just how snowy Colorado can get.

Wolf Creek Pass is one of the few major road crossings in southwest Colorado and is the major access point between southwestern Colorado and the rest of the state. Thus, it is easily accessible during the summer, and is a great place to finish or start your hike or to do a warm-up hike before doing another one of the hikes in this guide.

In this beautiful just-off-the-road hike, you get to experience one of the most iconic passes in Colorado. Walk along the longest mountain chain in the Rockies—the San Juans—with views of the South San Juans, a remote range known for landscapes unlike anywhere else on the CDT. In recent years, Wolf Creek Pass has become a ski area. This hike will take you near one of the most famous and picturesque skiing sites in Colorado.

Wildflowers on the Divide near Wolf Creek Pass.   PHOTO BY TERESA MARTINEZ

Note that snow can linger through this area until July. However, even in high snow years, this section tends to melt out and be passable by the third week of June. When snow obscures this trail, the CDT is much harder to follow. A map, compass, GPS, and the skills to use those tools are advised.

GETTING THERE: Take US 160 from Pagosa Springs for 23 miles north to Wolf Creek Pass. Alternately, you can take US 160 south from South Fork for 20 miles. Note that US 160 is steep (6.8 percent grade) and is often icy or snowy.

There is a large covered kiosk at Wolf Creek Pass describing the history of the Divide and the CDT. Just east of the pass, on the north side of the road, there is a gravel road, accessible to two-wheel-drive cars, that will take you to the Lobo Overlook. In 2015, CDTC volunteers installed a new trail kiosk at this site. This is a great place to start a hike as it brings you that much closer to the wilderness without having to do the climb—you can see Wolf Creek Pass right below you. There is ample parking near the microwave tower.

THE ROUTE: From the Lobo Overlook, walk west of the microwave tower to find the trailhead for the spur trail to the CDT. The trail is well worn and easy to follow. Generally

A storm rolling in near Wolf Creek Pass.   PHOTO BY TERESA MARTINEZ

head west and slightly downhill until the trail meets the CDT, which is marked by a post, 0.25 mile later.

Turn right onto the CDT. Climb slightly and then descend as you travel through lightly forested meadows for about 0.5 mile. Stay left at a trail junction as you continue to head downhill.

Climb to a sign marking the Weminuche Wilderness. About 0.5 mile later, descend to a low point that opens up into a meadow. From here, the CDT closely follows the Divide. Ascend back into the trees for about 1.0 mile, as you stay on the ridge. You will climb about 300 feet, sometimes on switchbacks, before contouring around 11,400 feet.

For the next mile you will still be heading west, traveling slightly north of the Divide. The terrain through here is light forest. You may cross a spring that forms the headwaters of a stream heading north. From there, the trail turns northwest, descending before reaching the southwestern shore of Rock Lake.

Although Rock Lake is relatively small compared to some of the lakes in the Weminuche Wilderness, its high elevation, accessibility, and the views from its shore make it quite memorable. A wooden hand-branded sign on a tree incorrectly reads "Lake Joyce." Take a break at the lake and retrace your steps back to your vehicle.

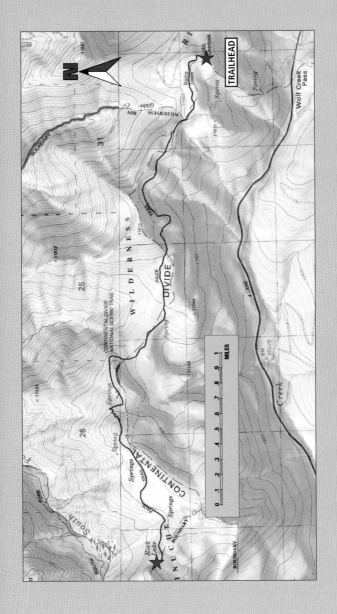

20. Cumbres Pass to Blue Lake

MAPS	Trails Illustrated, South San Juan/Del Norte, Number 142; Continental Divide Scenic Trail Map Book: Colorado, Bear Creek Survey, Segment 1, Map 1, Pages 34–35; Guthook App 794.8 to 821.7
ELEVATION GAIN	4,377 feet
RATING	Easy to moderate multi-day, difficult overnighter
ONE-WAY DISTANCE	32.6 miles (29.8 CDT miles)
ONE-WAY TRIP TIME	Overnighter, two days, or multi-day
NEAREST LANDMARK	Cumbres Pass Parking Area

COMMENT: This one-way car-shuttle hike starts at Cumbres Pass, near a station platform for the Cumbres & Toltec Scenic Railroad. The rail line was built in 1880 as part of the Rio Grande Railroad's southwestern extension to serve the silver mining districts of the South San Juans. Granted National Historic Status in 2013, the train now takes hikers, tourists, and history buffs between the towns of Chama, New Mexico, and Antonito, Colorado.

A unique feature of the Cumbres & Toltec Railway is that it was built to accommodate steam engines on narrow gauge rails. The rails on the line are three feet wide, rather than what became the standard in the United States, 4 feet, 8.5 inches. Plans were made to convert the rail lines to standard gauge, but it was not economically viable to do so after silver prices crashed in the wake of the Sherman Act of 1893. Today, train enthusiasts travel from around the world to marvel at this famed anachronism. The Cumbres & Toltec Railway is also notable for operating the last steam locomotive used for general freight service in the United States, a service that ended in 1969.

The South San Juans can be a green and lush paradise.

PHOTO BY PHIL "NOWHEREMAN" HOUGH

Although most of the track was dismantled, railway enthusiasts, preservationists, and local leaders were able to save the most scenic part of the line. In 1970, Colorado and New Mexico jointly purchased the rail, cars, yard, and maintenance facility. The railroad is now operated by the Friends of the Cumbres & Toltec Scenic Railroad. This non-profit organization's mission is "to preserve and interpret the railroad as a living history museum for the benefit of the public, and for the people of Colorado and New Mexico, who own it."

Your hike starts at Cumbres Pass, near the railway's halfway point between Chama and Antonito. Hikers can either drive or take the train to the pass to access some of the most isolated and scenic parts of the CDT in Colorado. Done as a daytrip, an overnighter, or a multi-day back-

In early season or in a big snow year, this section can be covered in snow.   PHOTO BY JOHNNY "BIGFOOT" CARR

packing trip, this hike offers stunning views of the South San Juan Wilderness, the Chama Basin, the drainages of the Conejos River, and, in the distance, the Sangre de Cristos Range.

In this uncrowded section of the CDT, hikers experience terrain very different from other places along the trail. Here, hikers seeking solitude walk along broad alpine plateaus strewn with lakes, some of which are regarded as the best fishing in the area. The plateau serves as the headwaters for Elk Creek, the South Fork of the Conejos, and Canon Verde—all major tributaries of the Conejos and Navajo Rivers, which are equally renowned for fishing. Each drainage has its own unique terrain and ecosystem and allows for many interesting side trips for hikers with enough extra time.

The route does not always have trail tread, but there are easy-to-spot large rock cairns marking the path. The hike is notable for fall colors in September and October as well as for herds of elk, whose haunting bugle fills the autumn forests. In summer, wildflowers abound in the numerous alpine plateaus that the CDT traverses. The last grizzly bear in Colorado lived in the South San Juans until it was killed in 1979. This wild section of trail sees few hikers, but offers big views.

GETTING THERE: The Cumbres Pass Trailhead can be accessed from the west by taking Colorado Hwy 17 about 8 miles north from Chama, New Mexico. Cumbres Pass can also be accessed from the east by taking US 285 to the town of Antonito, Colorado, and from there, driving west on Colorado 17 for 33 miles to just shy of the summit. There is a pullout on the south side of the road (right) that has five parking spaces. The CDT crosses Colorado 17 here, and the CDT south to New Mexico is near the pullout. (For this hike, those who park their cars on the south side will need to carefully cross Colorado 17 to the north side of the pass.)

Another option is to drive Colorado 17 from Chama past the railway station to the summit. Turn left onto Forest Service Road 118 at the turnoff to Trujillo Meadows Reservoir. Shortly after, turn left at the Y, following signs toward the CDT. The road heads west, passes right by the CDT trailhead marker (on the right), and crosses under the railroad trestle. The dirt road, where it dead-ends here, can be used as parking for five cars.

Alternately, you can take the Cumbres & Toltec Scenic Railroad from the town of Chama. CDTC members receive a discount on the ride. Check their website for train schedules.

To get to the Three Forks Trailhead: From the town of Monte Vista, drive 16 miles south on Colorado Hwy 15 to a signed turnoff for Platoro Reservoir. The road is also known as E. Co Road 12 S/Co Road Ff/Forest Development Road 250/Twelvemile Road. Follow this sign, heading west (right) on the windy road for 21 miles, where you will pass the Lost Elk Lodge and a small town with no services. Stay on Forest Development Road 250 (also called Alamosa Ave.) for 6.9 miles. Ignore a fork on the right (which leads to Forest Development Road 380 and Stunner Campground).

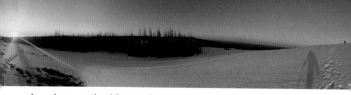

An early season thru-hiker watches sunrise from a snowy ridge.

PHOTO BY JOHNNY "BIGFOOT" CARR

Instead, continue south on Forest Service Road 250 for 3.3 miles to Stunner Pass. Continue 1.2 miles to a fork in the road and turn west (right) onto Forest Development Road 247. (Ignore signs for Mix Lake Campground or Skyline Lodge to your left.) Follow the western shore of Platoro Reservoir on Forest Development Road 247 for 4.0 miles. At the fork, stay left on what becomes Forest Development Road 245. Continue south on Forest Development Road 245 for 2.3 miles. The road dead-ends at the Three Forks Trailhead parking lot. There is a pit toilet at the lot. This route is also accessible from Pagosa Springs by taking Forest Service Road 667 to Elwood Pass for 28.1 miles, and then continuing onto Forest Development Road 380 until it hits Forest Development Road 247. Turn left on Forest Development Road 247, where you will meet the route mentioned above.

THE ROUTE: If you parked on the south side of Cumbres Pass, cross Colorado 17 and begin the hike at the northern side of Cumbres Pass on Colorado 17. The trail will spit you out at the small dirt parking area and a dirt road. Follow the road 0.1 mile until you cross under a railroad trestle. Immediately after, you will see the CDT Trail #813 trailhead and trail register on your left. Turn left onto the CDT. The first 3.0 miles of the hike are relatively flat, with mild undulations. As the trail contours and weaves through basins, you will pass four creeks and streams, the most notable being Wolf Creek, 3.4 miles into the hike. This part of your hike can be confusing because the trail crosses several dirt roads. Over the next 7.0 miles, the trail climbs about

2,000 feet to the Divide, skirting the Tierra Amarillo, an old Spanish land grant that has been private property for centuries.

The trail follows the plateau for 3.0 miles, traveling along the Divide, which marks the boundary between Archuleta County, to the west, and Conejos County, to the east. Around 6.0 miles into the hike, near a saddle, the trail comes very close to a road on the west and another trail to the east. Stay on the trail instead of taking the road.

About 8.0 miles into the hike, you will come into a semi-forested area. If you carried extra water here, or if there is snowmelt nearby, this may be a good place to camp. All surface water, including snowmelt, should be treated or purified before ingesting. Winds on the plateau can be strong and you may enjoy the protection the trees can provide your camp. Beetle kill is prevalent in this area so be sure to check trees near your camp for dead branches and trunks, which could fall on your tent at night.

At 15.5 miles into the hike, you will reach an intersection with the Flat Trail, which heads northeast to the Los Pinos Altos Trail. Continue north on the CDT to a high point at 12,187 feet and the South San Juan Wilderness boundary.

The trail descends from here and, 3.0 miles later, comes to an area with many small lakes. There is a trail intersection here—with the Dipping Lakes Cutoff Trail, which heads east. Continue along the CDT, which will be relatively flat along rolling alpine tundra for the next 5.0 miles, until you reach the two large Dipping Lakes. The trail crosses the lake's two inlets 19.5 miles into your hike. Although there is little tree cover at Dipping Lakes, it is a popular campsite for the few who travel this far. Be sure to camp at least 200 feet from water.

Shortly north of Dipping Lakes you will encounter a trail intersection with Elk Creek Trail #731, which leads to a campground and Forest Service Road 128 15.0 miles east. Stay on the CDT as it heads west and descends for 2.0 miles

Thru-hiker John Z. treks cairn to cairn in the snow just south of
Montezuma Peak.   PHOTO BY JOHNNY "BIGFOOT" CARR

to skirt the wilderness boundary. For the next 4.0 miles,
the trail contours just east of the Divide. You will pass two
trail intersections to the west. Shortly after an intersection
with the Valle Victoria, the trail travels just north of the
large Trail Lake.

After a high point, the trail descends into the trees, where
you will cross El Rito Azul. The trail continues west and
then north to your final destination along the CDT, Blue
Lake. From the lake, you can enjoy magnificent views of
Navajo Peak and the Navajo River drainage. This is an
excellent spot for a picnic or overnight stay. As always, be
sure to camp more than 200 feet away from the water and
avoid areas specifically closed to camping.

This is the end of this CDT segment, but your hike is not
over. From the southern part of the lake, follow trail signs to
the El Rito Azul Trail #718, indicating that Three Forks Park
is 3.5 miles away. This trail should take you east (right) away
from the CDT. After 0.25 mile on the El Rito Azul Trail,
ignore an intersection with the South Fork Trail #724, which
heads east. Continue north on the El Rito Azul Trail, which
travels through spruce forest and then along the west end of
a meadow near treeline. As you descend, the forest turns to
aspen. About 2.0 miles from the trailhead, you will have to
ford the Conejos River. Shortly after the ford, turn right and
enjoy easy walking along the Conejos River for 1.8 miles.
The trail ends at the south part of the parking lot.

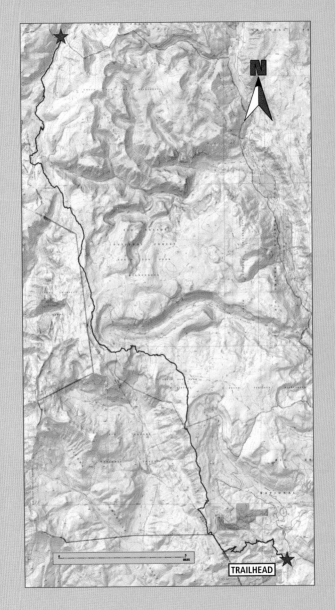

TRAILHEAD

About the Author

The Continental Divide Trail Coalition (CDTC) is the 501(c)(3) national nonprofit working in partnership with the US Forest Service, National Park Service, and Bureau of Land Management to protect, promote, and preserve the Continental Divide Trail. CDTC is a membership organization founded by a group of citizens passionate about the Continental Divide National Scenic Trail (CDNST) and working to building a strong community of supporters and trail enthusiasts who want to see the trail completed and protected, not just for today's users, but for future generations. CDTC's mission is to create a community committed to construct, promote, and protect in perpetuity the CDNST, which stretches from Canada to Mexico, through Montana, Idaho, Wyoming, Colorado, and New Mexico. CDTC is leveraging the strengths of its broad community of trail partners, local communities, enthusiasts, and supporters to build a strong coalition of support for the CDT so it remains a trail of not only national, but international significance. To learn more about CDTC or get involved, please visit www.continentaldividetrail.org and become a member, volunteer, or simply learn more about the 3,100-mile-long Continental Divide National Scenic Trail.

Liz Thomas thru-hiked the Continental Divide Trail from Canada to Mexico in 2010 and previously worked as the information specialist at the Continental Divide Trail Coalition. Among the most experienced female long-distance hikers in the country, Liz set the women's self-supported Appalachian Trail record in 2011 and has hiked over 15,000 miles on more than a dozen different long trails across the country. In her time not on trail, Liz attained a master's in environmental science degree from the Yale School of Forestry & Environmental Studies. She was honored with the prestigious Doris Duke Conservation Fellowship for her research on long-distance hiking trails, conservation, and trail town communities. Liz serves as vice president of the American Long Distance Hiking Association-West, the nonprofit that awards

Liz Thomas has also hiked the Pacific Crest Trail.

PHOTO BY NAOMI HUDETZ

hikers their "Triple Crown" upon completing the Appalachian Trail, the Pacific Crest Trail, and the Continental Divide Trail. Liz is the instructor of *Backpacker* magazine's Thru-Hiking 101 online course. This is Liz's first book.

Liz Thomas on the CDT.   PHOTO BY PAUL MAGNANTI